Ready Drafted Credit Control Letters and Forms

In an increasingly competitive world, it is quality of thinking that gives an edge – an idea that opens new doors, a technique that solves a problem, or an insight that simply helps make sense of it all.

We work with leading authors in the fields of management and finance to bring cutting-edge thinking and best learning practice to a global market.

Under a range of leading imprints, including *Financial Times Prentice Hall*, we create world-class print publications and electronic products giving readers knowledge and understanding which can then be applied, whether studying or at work.

To find out more about our business and professional products, you can visit us at www.business-minds.com

For other Pearson Education publications, visit www.pearsoned-ema.com

Ready Drafted Credit Control Letters and Forms

SECOND EDITION

Russell Bell

London • New York • San Francisco • Toronto • Sydney • Tokyo • Singapore •
Hong Kong • Cape Town • Madrid • Paris • Milan • Munich • Amsterdam

PEARSON EDUCATION LIMITED

Head Office:
Edinburgh Gate
Harlow CM20 2JE
Tel: +44 (0)1279 623623
Fax: +44 (0)1279 431059

London Office:
128 Long Acre, London WC2E 9AN
Tel: +44 (0)207 447 2000
Fax:+44 (0)207 240 5771
Website: www.business-minds.com

First published by Simon & Schuster in association with the Institute of Directors 1992

ISBN 0 273 64472 6 2nd edition
(ISBN 1 870555 579 1st edition)

British Library Cataloguing in Publication Data
A CIP catalogue record for this book can be obtained from the British Library.

Transferred to digital printing 2003

Typeset by Northern Phototypesetting Co Ltd, Bolton
Printed and bound by Antony Rowe Ltd, Eastbourne

The Publishers' policy is to use paper manufactured from sustainable forests.

About the author

Russell Bell is the Managing Partner of Stonehams, Solicitors and has been with the firm since 1972. He works in the Commercial Department specialising in Company Law including Sale and Purchase of Companies or business assets, Partnerships and re-structures, Intellectual Property (patents, trademarks, copyright, passing off), Contractual work including the sale and supply of goods and services, Venture Capital, Joint Venture and PFI, Asset Finance and Leasing and Franchising and Agency.

Russell instigated the formulation of the Quality Legal Group and founded the Croydon Business Awards. He sits on the council of the Institute of Directors and is an active member of Croydon Marketing and Development, the Croydon Professional Group, Business Link and Croydon Dining Club.

Russell may be contacted at:

Stonehams, Solicitors
Stoneham House
Croydon
Surrey CR0 1SQ
DX 2609 Croydon
Tel: 0208 681 2231
Fax: 0208 681 8324

Contents

Letters, forms and documents

Foreword

The need for effective credit control procedures is fundamental to the success of any business, whatever size and in whatever industry or sector they operate. It ensures a company not only survives in an increasingly competitive business environment, but more importantly, also provides a stable platform for growth.

A key element of any credit control strategy is credit insurance, and as the UK's largest credit insurer – with over £80 billion of trade underwritten each year – EULER Trade Indemnity recognises as well as anyone the value which credit controllers and managers bring to a business.

Our interest in – and understanding of – effective credit management is evidenced by a client base which includes many of the UK's leading businesses, from start-ups to multinationals based both in the British Isles and internationally.

Ready Drafted Credit Control Letters and Forms is a valuable contribution to an area of business practice which many companies still continue to neglect. It provides ready-drafted documents, letters and checklists covering every aspect of credit control.

More than this, it outlines the key elements within a credit control system, and provides useful tips and advice on early warning signals and making the most out of your procedures. This, together with legal advice, recommendations on making collections and alternative credit control techniques confirms this book as an important reference work which has become the standard textbook for credit controllers everywhere.

Jerry Friend
Commercial Director
EULER Trade Indemnity plc

Acknowledgments

Updating this book has been undertaken jointly by:

EULER Trade Indemnity	and the	Institute of Credit Management
1 Canada Square		The Water Mill
London		Station Road
E14 5DX		South Luffenham
		Oakham
		Leics
		LE15 9NB
Tel: 0207 512 9333		Tel: 01780 722912
Fax: 0207 512 9186		Fax: 01780 721333

Particular thanks are due to:

David Dhanoo Head of Legal and Policy Support

Tony Bushell Managing Director EULER Trade Indemnity Collections Ltd

Margaret Emmens Assistant Marketing Director

Particular thanks are due to:

Kate Beddington-Brown

We are also indebted to:

- Bruce Bosworth FICM
  Bosworth Associates
  22a Worcester Road
  Hagley, Stourbridge
  West Midlands DY9 0LD
  Tel: 01562 884810
  Fax: 01562 884259

  Bruce is a freelance consultant who specialises in credit management and business writing. Bruce kindly rewrote letters 1, 2, 3, 15, 16 (a) (b) (c), 18, 20, 21, 22, 25, 26, 27, 28, 29, 34, 36, 37 and helped to revise many of the remainder.

- Tony Ash FICM
  SLM Revenue Management Consultancy
  20 Searle Way
  Eight Ash Green
  Colchester
  CO6 3QS
  Tel: 01206 572999
  Fax: 01206 563322

  Tony is a freelance credit management consultant who generously gave his time and expertise to help with this project.

- The various ICM members who also worked hard to bring this initiative to fruition but wished to remain anonymous.

- NatWest.

- The Solicitors' Law Stationery Society.

Credit control systems

DO YOU NEED ONE?

It may come as something of a surprise to start a book on credit control by saying that every business already operates a cash control system of one kind or another.

We may be talking about a large organisation which retains substantial amounts of credit data on a highly technical computerised system, generating detailed reports on every aspect of its debtor lists, including detailed aged-debtor reports, particulars of the paying performance of each individual customer and the performance of each profit centre within the business. On the other hand, we may be talking about the businessperson who relies solely upon a regular and rather curt telephone message from his or her bank manager giving notice that once again the company is coming perilously close to the limit of its agreed overdraft facility, which then leads immediately to an urgent round of telephone calls and visits to customers for payment of overdue accounts.

In either of these cases, and in the range of variations in between, some form of 'system' exists, although some may be more organised and effective than others. The emphasis which is placed upon the need for a properly organised and efficient credit control system will depend to some extent on the market sector in which the business operates. If in that sector goods are delivered and services supplied on time, invoices are rendered promptly and payment is made on time without query or complaint, then everyone is happy and there may be no need to set up controls to ensure that cash is collected quickly. Whether such a market sector exists of course is extremely doubtful and those who are already operating in it will no doubt keep very quiet so as not to attract too much competition!

In most instances, however, payment by return cannot be guaranteed so some form of framework must be set up to ensure that the amount of money owed to the business by its customers does not get out of hand.

The nature of the system, its sophistication and the authority which its operators have will depend almost entirely upon whether the business leaders recognise a number of key factors. These are vital if any credit system is to make a significant contribution towards the survival and success of the organisation. They include the following:

1 The recognition of the vital role which cash as opposed to turnover or profits has in the day-to-day running of a business.
2 Awareness of the actual cost of providing extended credit lines and the effect that cost has on profit margins.
3 Recognition of the effect which unbudgeted delay in recovering debts due to a business has upon its liquidity.
4 Understanding the importance of providing appropriate authority to the company's credit managers to enable them to do their job properly and to contribute to the continued growth of the business.

The purpose of this book is to bring together and explain all these key elements and to summarise their importance at each stage of the collection process. It is also intended to provide, for small and medium-sized businesses in particular, a framework of forms, letters, contract terms and memoranda which will enable such businesses to set up their own internal systems and help them speed up the collection of cash owed to them, thus assisting survival and hopefully growth for the future.

Once these basic points have been taken on board the next step to be considered is how a straightforward yet efficient framework can be provided to enable a business to set up its own system of credit control. In its initial stages the system may have to operate on the simplest basis, perhaps using only a word processor and a diary, but later it may have to be built upon and the basic principles used in the development of the more sophisticated types of computerised systems described above. In either case, the framework must include:

- a method by which proper records are kept of each step in the credit management process;
- a recognition of the importance of written contractual terms and written confirmation of agreements which have been reached or promises made;
- the elimination of any opportunity on the part of your debtors to delay payment;
- prompt action in dealing with any complaints, queries or excuses which may be raised by your debtors to avoid or delay payment.

Before we can begin to construct a custom-made credit control system for your business, however, it is vital to ensure that the foundations are properly laid by some detailed consideration of the essential elements of effective credit management. We can now look at the first of these to see whether the correct attitude and approach prevails in your business to enable you to improve your cash collection performance.

The approach which has been adopted in this book is designed in the main to assist small and medium-sized companies which may not have substantial or particularly sophisticated accounting resources at their disposal and which may not already have a credit management team or an appointed individual within the organisation to carry out the credit management function. The basic principles which are advocated are, however, applicable to businesses of any size. In the first chapters the main issues to be faced by any organisation which is at all interested in the prompt and efficient collection of money due to it are addressed and broken down into manageable units which can be dealt with on a step-by-step basis. Guidelines are provided setting out the main points which must be understood by senior management if a proactive system is to be set up.

A basic framework is then advocated for the creation of such a system providing a number of documents, letters and checklists, running from the customer's initial application for credit to letters for use in the enforcement of any judgment which may have to be entered to enforce your contractual rights and remedies.

Each document is designed to perform a specific function but is also prepared in such a way as to be suitably adaptable to fit into the needs of your particular business. Explanations are given at each stage describing how each document fits in to the system as a whole and the principles which that document is intended to encompass.

It is entirely appreciated that the needs of each supplier will vary enormously depending upon the nature of the business, the market sector within which it operates, the volume of debts with which it has to deal and the resources which it has available to apply to the credit control process. It is hoped, however, that the basic principles and formulae which are recommended here will, subject to adaptation and refinement where necessary, provide a successful format within which any businessperson can begin to understand the credit control process and design a suitable method of credit organisation and collection for his or her own business. It should be emphasised of course that a number of the letters and documents described in this book are designed specifically to create or confirm legal obligations and on occasion they have particular reference to certain legal processes. In the event that you are in any doubt at all as to the ramifications of any of the documents referred to or the procedures advocated then professional advice should be sought.

THE IMPORTANCE OF CASH

The philosophy or underlying culture of a business, whether in the industrial or service sectors, will often depend on how that business has been developed over a number of years; perhaps more particularly, it depends on the influence exerted upon the business by certain individuals in the organisation at critical times. A company may adopt a cautious approach by growing organically, using capital and reserves generated by the sound management of its resources. Alternatively, it may go for growth by adopting the more risky route of merger and acquisition, funding those acquisitions by increased borrowing or by raising capital from outside sources. The personality of its leaders at any particular time and the approach they have to the decisions which are necessary to achieve survival and success, usually in that order, will clearly determine the course to be taken by the organisation and indicate whether a smooth or bumpy ride lies ahead.

For example, the impact of poor credit management both on individual companies and on whole industry sectors is substantial. A real-life case from EULER Trade Indemnity's credit management research illustrates the point.

The company concerned had an annual turnover of £1.5 million and a 5 per cent profit margin. Annual bad debt losses of £22,500 meant that the company had to generate additional sales of £450,000 if it was to recoup the profit lost because of the bad debt. This required an increase in sales of approximately 30 per cent.

The extent to which the influence of individuals controls a company's policies also applies to the way in which a company runs its day-to-day financial affairs and the emphasis which it puts on various aspects of its asset, resource and debt management. Again as an example, whether a company thinks it important to ensure that its debt/capital gearing or other financial ratios are in line with those adopted by its competitors in a specific industry will be determined principally by the approach of its senior executives. By the same token, the attitude of a company towards the recovery of money due to it can only be determined from the top. No matter how vigorous and diligent its credit managers may be, if the senior decision-makers of a business are lax or have their attention easily diverted elsewhere, whether towards marketing, production, or sales, then a general malaise will quickly develop downwards within the organisation. The business will soon find itself concentrating on the particular areas to which its leaders attach most importance, and if the recovery of debt is low on the agenda bad habits will soon creep in. Any credit disciplines already in place will be ignored and the morale of those responsible for credit control (if any) will quickly disintegrate. The company will soon be seen as something of an easy touch for even the most loyal customer, who in troubled times simply wants to take a bit of an advantage. Decision makers should bear in mind the following statistics:

- Trade debtors are an increasingly important asset accounting for an average 35 per cent of total assets.
- Less than 50 per cent of invoices are paid by the due date.
- Research has shown that 40 per cent of credit management time is spent on collecting overdue debts.

In general terms many businesspeople tend to aspire to one or more of four basic tenets as being the best targets to aim for in order to achieve commercial success in their particular field. They are:

- maximising sales;
- operating efficiency;
- profit making;
- cash flow management.

We have all seen enterprises in this country, some more publicised than others, whose leadership is so sales-orientated that nothing is allowed to stand in the way of the drive for turnover. In sporting terms the philosophy of such companies is 'provided that our team scores more than the opposition, then the game will be won in the end.' In the process the control of overheads is often ignored, profit margins are given scant attention and sales invoices are paid more or less at the customers' convenience. On no account must anything stand in the way of the corporate drive for increased sales and under no circumstances must customers be upset by pressure to pay for their purchases other than on the most relaxed payment terms. In such organisations the credit department (if one exists) is staffed by under-qualified managers and clerks who are the subject of friendly ridicule by the sales department who refer to them as the 'Sales Prevention Team'.

In growing markets such luxuries may be affordable, and continued growth in terms of sales can hide a multitude of sins as far as financial controls or lack of them are concerned. However, such luxury is likely to be enjoyed only in the short term. Sooner or later, as we have seen in recent years, a crunch will come and the business will usually find itself totally unprepared for the results, which will probably include increased borrowings, the disappearance of profits, a negative cash flow and possible insolvency.

Many of us have also seen, particularly during periods of fierce corporate takeover activity, the kind of enterprise in which the main talent has been directed towards cost savings and expenditure cuts. Such savings are often achieved after the acquisition of a new business by efficient cost management and reorganisation, and perhaps by the disposal of assets no longer required by the core business. Thus profits are created where little or none existed previously. In such businesses more attention is likely to be paid to the collection of cash, but again in extreme cases too much time and effort may be concentrated upon reorganisation or the disposal of assets which are not required, thereby bolstering the short-term turnover, profitability and cash flow of the basic business. The gains which are made can, perhaps justifiably, give rise to higher expectations from the company's shareholders and banks for future success. This in turn can lead to the urgent need for further acquisitions and disposals if the organisation is to generate further cash to pay its way. In other words, the business itself can change quite radically from being one which sells products or services into one which simply buys companies and sells assets.

Again, the continued success of such a policy in a business is dependent upon the ability of its leaders to continue along the acquisition trail, which may after a period of time diminish or peter out altogether. Target businesses may become more scarce, competition for them may become more intense, or the owners of the targets may be less willing to give themselves up for less than a worthwhile price once the acquirer's reputation in the market becomes known. If that happens and the management has not kept its house in order financially, the cost of borrowing and lack of attention to trading sales and cash flow will soon identify real problems in the business.

One would think that the third tenet, the pursuit of profit, would be quite unassailable as a doctrine of perfection. Profit after all has long been seen to be the motivating factor in most capitalist or market-led societies and it can be defined quite conveniently as the combination of the better aspects of the sales-orientated and cost-cutting philosophies. After all, if one is maximising sales and keeping overheads to a minimum, thus maximising profits, who is likely to complain?

Over-concentration on profits, however, can also lead to short-term delusion and long-term problems. Any enterprise which allows itself to be wooed by paper profits while ignoring the additional benefit of collecting cash will, sooner or later, appreciate that continued profit growth has become hampered by an inability to service that growth. That inability will have arisen directly from the company's failure to understand the benefit which it can achieve by realising quickly the profits it has worked so hard and so successfully to create. Paper profits are after all just that. They are simply numbers in a company's accounts and if they stay in that form they will do nothing at all to help the company pay its bills and remain in existence. After all, 'accounting profit' can be manipulated. Only cash flow statements give a true picture of a company's profitability.

During periods of economic growth, many businesses in all sectors, profitable and otherwise, fail to realise the lasting benefits of a continuously positive flow of cash. The efficient generation of cash by the swift conversion of marketing into sales and then the conversion of sales into paid invoices enables a business to reduce the cost of its borrowing, if such borrowing is required. It is able to expand its operations painlessly, to pay its own creditors promptly and therefore to negotiate advantageous terms, and it will win a popularity contest with any bank manager in the country. Such a business is also likely to be able to afford generous terms and benefits for its staff, enviable rewards for its directors, and attractive dividends for its shareholders.

One well-known adage is that 'cash is king', but a better analogy is to think of it as the 'lifeblood of industry'. Without cash, any form of growth will slow up, the energy levels required for success in a competitive market will wane, recovery from economic setbacks will become slower, eventually blackouts will occur and the patient may not survive the ordeal. There will also be a feeling of running extremely fast in trading terms just to stand still, together with a vague notion that others in leech-like fashion are living off the proceeds of your efforts. They are your debtors who fail to pay on time or at all.

By recognising the importance of cash, however, the businessperson who has recognised some of these symptoms may realise that the malaise which he or she originally complained about is perhaps more general than first thought. By the introduction of a committed philosophy of credit control the haemorrhaging process can be reversed and a healthily positive cash flow can be maintained. Before that can happen, however, some hard facts may have to be faced and lessons learned if a true commitment is to be achieved.

THE COST OF CREDIT

Although some attitudes in British business have changed during recent years, many firms still do not pay sufficient attention to credit control. Credit control is still regarded in too many companies as being solely connected with the collection of debts, an operation which comes into effect only when the customer has been invoiced and payment is overdue. Frequently, even in some of the larger and more prominent of our corporations the credit control department consists of a manager and three or four clerks, responsible in turn to an assistant accountant who is some way distant from board responsibility. The result is that the credit function of the company has no representation at director level and there is little interest in the effect that its efficiency or lack of it has on company profits and financial strategy. That attitude will prevail until something goes wrong and cash becomes an urgent requirement.

What many businesses fail to realise is that the marketing and sales operations do nothing more than convert products or services into invoices. Leaving the conversion of invoices into cash more to luck than to good judgement does nothing at all to keep the business alive and well. Similarly, the notional profits which arise as a result of good cost control and efficient marketing are only of any relevance to the business, its directors, shareholders and creditors when the invoices are converted into cash and placed in the bank.

Unfortunately, it is the very system of converting sales into cash which is overlooked by the managers of many companies today. Directors would do well to remember that every £10,000 a year that a company loses in bad debts is £10,000 that could have been reinvested or could have contributed to increased competitiveness. The 'opportunity cost' of bad debt can be quite substantial, quite apart from the amount of catching up that needs to be done as a consequence.

Such an approach is often the result of a lack of understanding in corporate leaders of the role that efficient and positive credit management can take in the running of a business. It also displays a clear lack of appreciation of the cost to that business when credit is offered to or taken by customers over an extended period.

The cost of credit is quite easy to calculate. Assuming that you pay interest to your bank at the rate of 12 per cent per annum for your overdraft facility, then any invoice which is overdue for one month will add 1 per cent of the invoice price to your costs.

This will have a direct effect on the profitability of the sale in question and reduce the profit on that sale by an identical amount.

Bearing in mind that most British companies operate on net profit margins before tax of 5 per cent of turnover or less, it can be readily appreciated that if the above costs are not taken into account in the pricing policies of such businesses, then profit margins can rapidly diminish in the absence of the prompt and regular collection of cash.

If the average time for collection for invoices is in fact 90 days and inflation is running at the rate of 9 per cent per annum, then you will be able to calculate that by the time payment has been made after three months, bank interest of 3 per cent of the invoice value will be due and inflation of 2.25 per cent will have arisen. The 5 per cent average net profit level will have been overtaken completely by the combined effects of the costs of borrowing and the rigours of inflation. At that stage running fast to stand still does not come into it – the company is running fast and going backwards!

Of course, allowing extended terms of credit can be used as a tool by which turnover can be increased by attracting more business. It is vital, however to recognise the real cost of allowing extended credit and to adjust prices accordingly to take into account the effects described above. It is possible that the additional turnover and profit which may be generated by deliberately allowing customers to buy products on extended credit terms will outstrip the costs. It is up to managers of the business to ensure that the combined effect of extended credit, and perhaps increased prices to cover the costs involved, are sufficient to generate higher profits on any increased sales. The higher the interest you have to pay and the higher the current rate of inflation the worse will be the effect on profits. The long-term benefit to the company of increasing sales by giving longer terms of credit will seem more and more doubtful.

Much will depend upon the company's ability to sustain its market share and level of sales while it increases its prices to cover the period of extended credit allowed. At the same time, it must ensure that the terms of credit it has settled upon are rigidly adhered to so that no more hidden or unconsidered costs creep in.

By not taking all these factors into account, the managers of the business are in effect 'flying blind'. They are without the basic information needed in order to judge whether they are creating sufficient turnover at the right prices to cover their overheads, or generating sufficient cash income from their sales effort to keep the company going. How then can they ensure that they are keeping their customers happy, meeting the terms offered by the competition and maintaining control of their cash collection?

EXTENDED CREDIT AND LIQUIDITY

Liquidity is basically the means by which an enterprise's assets are converted into cash to enable the business to generate sufficient funds to pay for its day-to-day liabilities as they fall due. Raw materials purchased have to be converted into products, or staff time converted into services, and those products and services have in turn to be converted into sales before they can result in cash income for the company. That cash in turn is then converted back into raw materials or staff time and the whole process begins again. The more speedily that cycle turns, then on the assumption that on each turn there is a marginal profit, the greater the company's profits will be and the higher will be the level of cash generated.

If a delay occurs at any of the conversion stages, that is to say if raw materials purchased sit around for a long time before being converted into stock, if stock is left on the shelf for considerable periods before being converted into sales, or if sales are allowed to stagnate before being converted into cash, then the end result will be that the business will begin to fail because it is not generating sufficient cash income to pay its way. This will result in 'cash flow problems' which simply means that the company is not generating sufficient cash income on a week-by-week or month-by-month basis. Difficulties will arise in meeting the wages, rents, raw materials, hire purchase repayments and other overheads which have to be paid out of revenue to keep the company going. In the end the whole process grinds to a halt and the business folds when insufficient funds are generated to pay debts as they fall due and insolvency looms.

Normally, of course, the companies which concentrate their efforts on sales turnover, cost cutting or paper profits are those upon whom the rigours of cash deficiency creep up with the least notice. Their only tool for measuring the liquidity of their position is their bank statement and quite often the real focus for their attention, namely the fact that their overdraft facility has been exceeded or the bank draws attention to the problem by returning cheques, comes too late for any effective action to be taken.

This position is bound to arise if cash flow forecasts are not produced on a regular basis, debtor levels are allowed to increase to an unacceptable position and the liabilities of individual customers are not properly monitored. It is often said that the principal objective of business is to achieve profit, but we have already seen the fallacy in such a statement if left in isolation. If the objective of business is to achieve sales turnover and profit, then the objective of proper credit management must be to convert that sales turnover into cash as quickly as possible. The ideal, therefore, is to attain the highest level of sales possible at the best profit margins achievable but to have payment for those sales outstanding for the shortest possible time. In this way the revenue which goes from those sales into the bank will be maximised, thereby creating cash for the company to carry on and to expand its business. Let us see how that can be done on a sensible and economic basis.

The value of the written word

For thousands of years men and women have endeavored to find ways to perfect methods of communication between themselves. Words are now processed, faxed, e-mailed, laser-printed or transmitted by satellite but there are still those among us who prefer to keep our words as imprecise and vague as possible and certainly try to avoid writing anything down at all costs!

Part of the reason for such behaviour is the notion that if a detailed record is not taken of an agreement, an exchange of views or some other form of discussion, then perhaps it did not really happen at all, or at least the terms of that agreement or conversation can be denied or varied at some later date. Under English law, however, and in a great many other jurisdictions around the world which have followed the English legal system, oral agreements are perfectly enforceable and oral terms can vary the provisions of a written contract.

The upshot of this is simply that by failing to record properly and to commit to writing the terms of a contract or the areas covered by a discussion, the parties involved do not escape the rigours of English contract law. All they do is create uncertainty for the future.

Of course, some people in business prefer things that way and feel that if they are given appropriate opportunity they can slide out of their contractual obligations if no accurate record has been kept. On other occasions, the motivation is more innocent and is driven by a feeling that to confirm the terms of a conversation by letter or to write down details of a telephone conversation is somehow ungentlemanly. This attitude stems from an era when the popular adage was 'an Englishman's word is his bond' and although such high moral principles are still greatly desirable, no doubt most of our commercial friends would prefer to have the Englishman's bond!

Reluctance to rely on the written word can also be caused by laziness. If one imagines a telephone conversation when contractural terms are being discussed, there can be a tendency to deal with the points which are agreed or capable of agreement and which are therefore easier to cope with. It is also much easier in those circumstances to skip over the more contentious terms or those which require more determined negotiation. The end result is that if a letter is not sent from one party to the other confirming, for example, that the quantities and prices of products have been agreed but that a delivery schedule has not, the two parties to the same conversation may have distinctly different recollections of what has and has not been agreed. If one party or the other is later dissatisfied with the performance of that contract, then they could both quite easily finish up as the plaintiff and defendant in expensive and time-consuming court proceedings without the benefit of any accurate account of their agreement to help them decide the issue.

It is often the case that the actual value of writing letters giving notice, confirming rights, creating obligations or denying liabilities may be more psychological than anything else. They can have the effect of enforcing in the minds of the parties concerned the points which have been agreed or disputed during oral discussions, whether those discussions have taken place on the telephone or at formal meetings. It can be equally important to keep accurate personal records of meetings or conversations, provided that such notes are taken or prepared at or very shortly after the discussion takes place. If in the course of subsequent negotiations one party has on file a record of the discussions, whether in manuscript or typed form, and if more particularly a letter has been written to his or her opposite number on each occasion with a minute or other form of record of the conversation or meeting, then even if the use of those records does not provide sufficient leverage in the course of negotiations to persuade the other side to accede to one's recollection, they will still provide valuable evidence in the event that the parties find themselves in court arguing out the detailed issues which remain between them.

Most if not all of these problems can be avoided by the prompt exchange of properly drafted business letters. There can be many purposes or reasons for writing such letters but the main ones would appear to be as follows:

- to elicit a response;
- to give notice of an intention;
- to confirm rights;
- to create obligations;
- to deny liabilities;
- to provide evidence.

A letter written to elicit a response will require some form of specific reply from the person receiving it. To be effective, the request should be clear and concise and preferably give some indication of a timescale within which the response is required. The requirement of a person who says

> Please send your cheque to be received by [date]

is more precise and understandable than one who simply says

> You owe me money

or even requests the cheque to be sent 'by return'.

Of course, to be effective such letters must be followed up promptly if the required response is not received. A simple diary system can work efficiently provided one is clear about the next step to be taken.

> Please send me your cheque to be received by [date] or I will instruct my solicitors to take legal action

is perfectly clear in all respects.

Business letters can also be used to give notice of one's intentions, particularly in circumstances where the right to take certain action already exists subject to the giving of proper notice. For example:

> We hereby give you notice that our prices will increase by 5 per cent as from the 1st of [month]

is perfectly clear and places both parties in a position of knowing exactly where they stand. The sender has probably fulfilled the conditions of his or her own terms of trading and the recipient knows exactly what his or her position is and can decide whether to place further orders or not. Compare this with a telephone conversation when one party indicates to another that prices are likely to increase at some unspecified date in the future and then when goods are ordered simply invoices the customer at the higher rate. The customer, having relied on an earlier price list, feels that he or she has to some extent been duped or has been given inadequate notice of the supplier's intentions, while the supplier may feel that sufficient notice has been given of his or her intentions and if the customer wanted further details he or she could have asked! The uncertainty of the latter position is entirely unsatisfactory for commercial purposes and will again only lead to future conflict. It must be appreciated that for a party to rely on a particular term in a contract, English law requires that 'reasonably sufficient notice' of that term be given to the other party before or at the time when the contract is concluded.

The confirmation of legal or contractual rights is one of the most beneficial but least used purposes of letters and memoranda. Only a formal contract signed by both parties is more effective than a letter or note stating:

> I confirm our recent telephone conversation when we agreed that there was no dispute arising on the following invoices and that you would make payment within seven days [list the date and value of each unpaid invoice]. You also accepted that if such payment was not made we would have the right to sue you for the full balance remaining plus interest and costs.

Such a note is not eliciting a response or giving notice of an intention. What it is doing is confirming a certain position and unless the recipient of the letter writes back promptly to deny the writer's version of the conversation on the telephone and to deny the rights which are claimed, then the principal inference will be that the letter records correctly the terms which have been accepted by both parties. This provides extremely useful ammunition in the event that payment is not received and legal proceedings become necessary.

In a similar manner such correspondence can be used to create obligations on the part of the recipient which may not previously have been accepted. The use of words such as:

> I note that you have failed to deliver the goods ordered on 1 June within 14 days as agreed. That order is therefore cancelled and I require the repayment of my refundable deposit by return

can have the effect of creating an obligation on the part of the recipient if a reply is not sent out very quickly denying the facts alleged or raising a counter-argument against the conclusions reached. Obviously, the recipient of a letter of this nature may not have written voluntarily to confirm the new obligation placed upon him or her and so it is almost always incumbent upon the party wishing to create the obligation to write promptly, clearly setting out the terms he or she believes apply, thus avoiding any confusion in the future. If the recipient wishes to object to the terms which are recorded he or she must do so promptly, and preferably in writing. A telephone call, no matter how irate, can always be denied later. Although to many businesspeople this procedure may feel awkward and perhaps unnecessary, it can of course lead to an early clarification of the issues between the parties and an earlier resolution of their difficulties.

For the same reasons, as soon as any liability is alleged either in the course of conversation or by the kind of correspondence that has been described above, it is very important that a strong and clear denial of those liabilities is dispatched as a matter of urgency.

Say, for example, in a telephone conversation between your customer and your accounts department, an allegation is made that your goods are not up to scratch or that delivery has been late and has resulted in loss to your customer. If those facts are to be denied, then apart from the initial oral response, it is extremely helpful to have on file a letter which first of all records the complaint and secondly confirms that having inspected the goods or checked your own records the point which has been raised is denied. At the same time your claim for payment can be repeated! Without that denial your customer is left with a feeling at least that some point has been won and at best that there is on record some form of notice of liability on your part which, since it has gone without response, has in some way enhanced his or her moral or contractual position.

At the end of the day, if there is still substantial dispute as to what has been agreed and what has not and a settlement cannot be achieved, the ultimate arbiter may be a County Court or High Court judge who will be confronted by two parties who have different recollections of the same conversations or the same meetings. Inevitably, the judge will be swayed one way or the other, not only by the demeanour of the witnesses in court but also by their commercial efficiency. To some extent this boils down to the manner in which records have been kept of meetings, the way in which agreements have been recorded and the promptness with which legal rights and obligations have been confirmed in correspondence between the parties and pursued subsequently. If one side has continually kept accurate minutes and memoranda of discussions and has written to the other side on a regular basis confirming agreements reached, while the other has neglected all of these steps but has simply relied on vague recollections of conversations and meetings which have taken place months if not years before, then there will be virtually no contest. In the course of any negotiations, or in pleading a case before a judge in court, the pressure will always be on the party without documentary evidence to confirm his or her credibility and the assumption will remain that the party whose records are confirmed, contemporaneous and up to date is in the right.

Identifying problems

EARLY WARNING SIGNS

Having considered the importance of cash flow to the survival of a business and the importance of documentary evidence to support or fend off claims as they arise, we can now look at what can happen if these areas are ignored and the business of a company is allowed to run itself without suitable controls and systems in place to enable its managers to operate profitably.

Of course, good managers will have the right combination of vision, experience and organisational skills to ensure that they are in control and that they are anticipating problems before they arise rather than reacting to them on a firefighting basis. Other managers, however, may lack the experience which is necessary to provide such foresight, or indeed they may have inherited problems which have been caused by the negligence or inabilities of others and which they have been left to resolve. The important thing is to be able to recognise the symptoms before real problems arise and to take the necessary remedial action to avoid them or minimise their effect.

Financial problems can manifest themselves in a large number of ways, some of which may be identified as follows.

Hitting the overdraft limit

Regularly bumping along the ceiling of your banker's credit facility, perhaps with the embarrassment of the occasional returned cheque, leaves the business vulnerable either to a further slowing of cash funds – say when a major customer defaults – or to the withdrawal or reduction of facilities which your bank may review on a quarterly or six-monthly basis.

Extended aged-debtor lists

A company's credit terms may require payment by its customers within 30 days from the date of invoices, but if payment of such invoices takes on average between 70 and 90 days as is the case with many businesses in the United Kingdom, then clearly the cash collection system is not working or there are other problems which have to be identified.

Good payers slowing up

If a company finds that its regular customers who have paid promptly and within contractual terms in the past are slowing their payments and contributing towards the aged-debtor position, then again this may be a warning sign either that the customers have their own problems or that they have recognised that the company's collection system is slack and allows some leeway despite the terms for payment originally agreed.

Quality complaints

Some complaints may be spurious if the company's customers begin to take advantage of an inefficient system, or if they see that complaints about products or services or queries about accounts or invoices are not dealt with promptly. They will then be able to use any kind of complaint or query to slow up the collection process and take advantage accordingly, improving their own cash flow as a result.

Administrative excuses

We have all come across the old chestnuts, such as 'computer failure', 'changing bank accounts', 'absence of cheque signatories' and 'inability to find a copy of the original invoice' as excuses for non-payment or delayed payment of invoices which are properly due. Some of these may be genuine but in many cases they are simply a sign that the company's customers have recognised that the company's credit system is lax and capable of exploitation. If appropriate records are kept and the right system is in place, however, those excuses will be quickly recognised and resolved.

Customer insolvencies

On a one-off basis most businesses can survive the insolvency of a customer provided they have not allowed that customer to build up debts which on default would seriously affect their own solvency. On the other hand, if the company is too heavily reliant on the business of one particular customer, or is involved in a market sector where insolvencies are frequent during times of recession, or if it is dealing with a range of customers who are vulnerable in cash flow terms, then the company must take steps urgently to ensure that it has adequate protection. This can either take the form of a strong internal system of credit risk assessment and categorisation which enables the company to monitor its debtor list and credit limits, or alternatively some form of credit insurance which, while providing a general form of indemnity for such losses, would also impose a measure of organisation and discipline into the company's affairs. We will be considering both these options later.

Supplier stops

This is an almost identical problem to hitting the overdraft limit on a regular basis but refers instead to the supply of stock for the company's purposes rather than the supply of cash from its bank. If the company is not paying its bills and its suppliers are operating an efficient credit control system with defined credit limits, then at some point in time invoices will become overdue, credit limits may be exceeded and supplies refused as a result, causing considerable disruption to the company's ability to generate turnover, profits and, of course, cash.

Credit ratings and market rumours

If as a result of a decline in profits and inefficiencies in the collection of cash the company finds itself in a position where it cannot fund further purchases of stock, the immediate result is an inability to supply all its own customers. Turnover drops, margins become affected by the high interest rates it has to pay on its borrowings, profits are reduced as a direct result, collection of cash is reduced to a trickle and suppliers cannot be paid. This downward spiral of trading is then reflected in a rapid marking down of the company's credit ratings, which in turn is quickly picked up within the company's market place. Rumours abound, suppliers and customers alike become nervous and refuse to take or place orders, and business declines even further.

Arrears of PAYE, NIC, VAT

Quite often, when a business is struggling to survive, the state is the creditor from whom indulgence is first sought. After all, staff have to be paid, the bank will have set its own limits, and suppliers must be encouraged to keep stock flowing inwards. The British tax authorities, however, while tightening their own collection procedures considerably during recent years, are still seen as providing an opportunity to improve a company's cash position by non-payment. Obviously, this is a short-term measure which the authorities will not tolerate. The use by a number of government departments nowadays of various summary methods for the enforcement of debts, such as the immediate seizure of assets, stock and equipment by court bailiffs, provides another example of how problems can arise, ostensibly without warning.

Cuts in non-productive budgets

Frequently, the first budgets to go are those which are perceived to be making little or no contribution to a company's profitability, or are seen as something that can be dispensed with in the short term and picked up again later. Therefore, we often see the marketing, training, personnel or legal departments of larger companies cut substantially during times of trading difficulty, and in smaller companies the budgets for marketing, training or legal activities are significantly reduced. On occasion, however, those cuts can be counterproductive, if, for example, the marketing of a company's services is essential to the acquisition of business, the achievement of profits and the generation of cash, or if the continuous training of staff is vital to the quality of the products or services supplied.

Low staff morale

All these difficulties inevitably have a direct effect on the way the company's employees feel about the business generally. Returned cheques are seen by the accounts department, supplier stops are noted by the production department, marketing cuts are noticed immediately by the sales department, and a visit by a bailiff in pursuit of a tax bill is seen by everyone! The result of this is low staff morale, high staff turnover as the company's better employees start to leave the sinking ship, and a degree of interdepartmental strife as staff who have been loyal team members begin to bicker between themselves to find someone to blame.

Of course, many of the above problems and examples are anecdotal and while there are a number of more scientific methods which enable the management of companies to identify and resolve such problems before they arise, as often as not the main problem is with the management itself. If they are too complacent within their own market place, or lack the ambition to drive the company forward, or are generally satisfied with the performance of an under-achieving business, then they are unlikely either to recognise the symptoms appearing before them or to have the determination necessary to carry out the remedial work which may be required. Good managers, if they recognise the problem early enough, may be able to deal with the difficulties by the application of some preventative medicine which, while being rather unpalatable, is still capable of bringing the business round. The only alternative, if things are left rather too long, would be major surgery, including perhaps corporate restructure and disposals which could be even less attractive for the company in the short term. The final outcome, however, if neither of these options is taken up in sufficient time, will be terminal decline resulting in the demise of the business sooner rather than later.

How then can the management of a business avoid these difficulties? Having taken on board the principal points raised earlier, namely the recognition of the value of cash to its enterprise and the importance of maintaining proper written records of the company's transactions and agreements, the management may also recognise some of the warning signs in the company's current performance that we have already considered. The next step is to begin to set up an efficient, productive and positive credit control system which will avoid the more obvious pitfalls in future.

AVOIDING DEFICIENCIES, SOLVING PROBLEMS

As soon as a business begins to see any of the warning signs which have been mentioned, it is vital that its managers take urgent steps to review the company's position, to identify the areas in which the problems are arising and to put in place a system which will avoid the recurrence of those problems. The key element involved in the provision of such systems, however, is the recognition that the prompt collection of cash is vital for the survival of the business and any aid or assistance which can be brought to bear to that end must be carefully considered and quickly put into force.

Once management has successfully spotted its problems, its next task is to identify what deficiencies are arising, to review the company's procedures for dealing with those deficiencies (if any) and where possible to set up appropriate systems or practices to provide the required remedy. The areas to be tackled may include:

- the assessment of credit risk;
- the methods by which cash is collected;
- the market in which the company is operating;
- the types of customer the company has to deal with;
- the terms upon which the company is accustomed or obliged to trade.

A positive collection system

It is all too easy to think that in order to achieve any success in improving a company's collection performance its credit managers must be overbearing and perhaps even threatening in the eyes of its customers. That approach has, however, become increasingly old-fashioned in recent years. It is now commonly felt that the best way to achieve success in the management of credit is to have all the necessary information at your disposal in order to be able to conduct the collection process in a positive manner and then to use that information within a system which can provide the maximum benefit to your business. Many companies are now combining the collections and customer service functions, e.g. making a customer service call to ensure that the goods/services were to the customer's satisfaction. This, in effect, removes any excuse not to pay.

In addition, there is the need to acquire basic information about your customers, such as:

- recognising whether they can afford to pay your charges;
- being aware of the date upon which they produce their cheques each month to pay your invoices;
- knowing the cheque signatories which your customers have to have present in order to sign valid cheques in your favour;
- identifying the staff member responsible for passing invoices for payment;
- identifying habitual poor payers.

By using this kind of information properly, and by ensuring that any queries on your invoices are avoided and that any complaints arising in relation to the products or services you have supplied are dealt with promptly and efficiently, you will be able to avoid supplying customers who are bound to default, or unnecessarily antagonising good customers who already have your payment in the pipeline within their own procedures. You will also be able to ensure that delays arising as a result of queries or complaints on your invoices are kept to an absolute minimum.

Remember that a negative attitude towards cash collection will result in a negative response from your customers. If they feel threatened, or if they feel that your system is inefficient, then they will respond in kind by putting your invoices at the bottom of the pile for payment, or by raising spurious excuses for non-payment which they know your system will not be able to cope with promptly. An efficiently organised credit system on the other hand will avoid giving the customer any reason for delaying payment or refusing to pay. Once your customers get the message, the system can actually encourage them to put your invoices at the top of that pile, or if you can get them working in your favour, actually bring forward your account for early or favourable treatment in special cases.

Know your customers

In the course of your dealings with a particular company you will acquire an enormous amount of information about that company's own procedures, which if properly used can enable you to provide a better service for that customer's needs while at the same time engendering a positive approach from your customer towards your own requirements. The kind of information that should be retained will include:

- the identity of the individuals in the customer organisation who process and approve your invoices;
- the identity of the individuals who prepare and sign the cheques which are sent out to pay you;
- the latest date in each month when you can send your invoices in sufficient time to ensure that they will be checked, approved and signed off in time for your customer's next cheque run;
- whether your customer pays within your terms of credit or whether he or she insists on extended terms;
- whether you have ever had to threaten or take legal proceedings to recover overdue accounts from that customer;
- which bank your customer uses and his or her standing there;
- what tangible assets your customer has and where they are kept, including property, stock and equipment;
- any rumours or press comments which may be picked up about your customer's trading profitability or otherwise.

Risk assessment

The most important piece of information you can know about your customers is whether or not they have the ability to pay! Lack of current credit data on customers and substantial credit exposure to those customers is a common cause of serious cash flow difficulties for many companies, particularly when those customers themselves become vulnerable or insolvent. It is therefore vital to be aware of any constraints which your own customers may be facing in financial terms. Their creditworthiness must be assessed at an early stage (preferably before any trading commences or credit terms are agreed) and reviewed regularly, and if necessary strict limits on any credit lines should be imposed and enforced. All too often the competition running between the sales department and the credit management team centres on this particular area and in order to keep a long-established customer happy credit limits are overridden or ignored completely. The consequence of this is that your company itself becomes vulnerable to a form of financial blackmail. This can take the form of a clear indication that if too much pressure is brought to bear to recover money due, then the customer will take his or her business elsewhere or that such pressure will force the business under, or even worse that if further supplies are not allowed, then that too will drive the customer into insolvency. As often as not if the original credit limits had been properly assessed and applied those problems would not have become nearly so severe.

Remember:

- over a quarter of business failures are long-standing, previously prompt-paying customers;
- one company fails every few minutes of every working day.

Using enforceable contractual terms

For obvious reasons the contractual terms upon which parties may wish to trade will differ depending upon their role in any particular transaction. A purchaser will insist upon certain terms applying with regard to the timing of delivery, the pricing of the goods or services bought, or the implied statutory conditions under the Sale of Goods Act 1979, Supply of Goods and Services Act 1982 and Sale and Supply of Goods Act 1994 which are normally applied to the commercial supply of goods and services. These include the provision that any goods sold will be of satisfactory quality and fit for their designated purpose, that the seller should be the proper owner of the goods he or she is selling, and that goods sold by description or sample will comply with the description which was given or the sample previously supplied.

The seller, on the other hand, will be trying to limit his or her exposure both in financial and contractual terms by setting out the date by which payment is expected, by trying to have some degree of tolerance with regard to delivery schedules or the amount of goods to be supplied under the contract, or perhaps limiting his or her potential liabilities under any warranties or guarantees which have been given or under the implied statutory conditions mentioned above.

All of these issues can be dealt with properly provided that the contractual terms between the parties are clearly set out and properly documented and agreed in advance. Problems only arise where insufficient attention has been paid to the contractual basis upon which the goods or services are being supplied, or in the case of the seller if he or she is too keen on achieving the sale at any cost and does not insist upon properly recording the terms of supply. The end result when that seller is trying to recover money due will be constant queries from the purchaser with regard to the terms and timing of delivery, the pricing and condition of goods after delivery and the time for payment of invoices which have been delivered. Again, all this does is to give more and more opportunity to customers to delay payment and to slow down your company's cash flow.

Training your staff

The credit manager and his or her team must be given proper status within the organisation. The credit manager should be accountable to a director of the company of equal or higher status to the sales director, and other departments within the organisation should be made fully aware of the importance of the credit management team in collecting the cash due to the company and therefore ensuring its survival. It must be emphasised time and again that while the production team turns raw material into products and the sales team turns those products into turnover, that turnover remains as a book entry only until the credit management team turns that book entry into cash, thus enabling the company to discharge its own debts, to pay its staff and to remain in existence.

In addition, the credit management staff must be properly trained. They should be given proper tuition in order to carry out all the tasks required of them and be provided with resources to do their job properly. You will find, however, that your investment will be more than adequately rewarded by the additional stimulus your business will receive from a positive collection team and the cash income they can generate.

Ensure coordinated effort

Once appropriate status has been given to your credit manager and his or her staff, it is important that they too recognise the vital roles that have to be taken by other players in the corporate team. Without *Research and Development* the company's goods may never be suitably designed to hold a place in the market. Without efficient *Purchasing* the company may always be working at margins less than those of its competitors. Without proper *Marketing* the company's customers may never get to know about the excellent products it has to offer. Without efficient *Production* the goods may not live up to the design qualities envisaged or the promises of the marketing team. Without a proper *Sales* organisation the prospects created by marketing may never be exploited to the full. Unless *Despatch* delivers the goods on time and in one piece to the company's customers the company will never be paid. And without an efficient *Accounts* department invoices will not be delivered accurately or to the right place at the right time, and again excuses for late or non-payment will be created.

Of course, if all the other members of the team are operating at 100 per cent efficiency then there must be a strong temptation for suggesting that the role of the credit management team can be played down or reduced by a significant degree. That would be a big mistake. The credit manager should be in a position where he or she is acting as a sounding board for the whole company and perhaps more particularly as a source of constant feedback from the company's customer. If the job is being done properly and the credit manager is in constant contact with customers at the right level and in a positive manner, he or she will be the first one to learn if the R&D department has fallen down on design, if the promises of the marketing team are not being kept, if production is failing to manufacture within reasonable tolerances, if the sales representatives are making promises they cannot keep, if despatch is not delivering on time and if accounts are sending out invoices which are inaccurate.

On the other side of the fence, the credit manager will be keeping a close eye on his or her customers, in particular their performance with regard to the prompt payment of invoices as they fall due and their ability to pay for further goods and services delivered. Every effort will be made to ensure that trading continues within credit limits set and that any queries raised in relation to trading between the company and the customer are genuine and promptly dealt with.

All departments from Research and Development through to Credit Control are like the spokes of a wheel. They all give strength to the wheel to enable it to revolve smoothly. If one spoke weakens or fails, the wheel becomes unstable and may collapse. To enable the credit manager to function effectively, however, some basic tools must be provided and we can now look at what documents, letters and other written ammunition we can put at his or her disposal to assist in this task.

Avoid panic measures

When a business begins to meet difficulties in its cash flow the pressures which are brought to bear by its bankers, its suppliers and ultimately its shareholders can mean that the directors are often forced into taking short-term measures which may result in only short-term gains. Collection purges during which the credit management team is instructed to telephone every customer whose account is more than 30 days old can often be a waste of time if the problem accounts are not properly targeted. While every account outstanding for more than the time indicated by the company's contractual terms is strictly overdue, the amount of effort needed to chase one debt of, say, £100 is probably no more or less than that required to recover a debt of £10,000, but the respective benefits to the company upon a successful collection will be obvious.

In addition, if the company's collection methods are still negative and aggressive and are still based on insufficient or inaccurate information, then it may well be that customers who are paying quite properly within their own terms for payment are being driven away by such methods at a time when the company needs all the trade it can get. Again, it is question of organisation and control. In the forms and letters which are set out and explained in this book various methods of achieving a properly organised credit control system are advocated. The aim is to provide a framework within which a properly timed, coordinated and controlled system of collection can be put into place. If properly organised and executed, this system can take your company to a position where it is recognising the benefits of properly managed credit control, enable it to create and maintain its own system effectively and allow it to enforce its rights quickly and efficiently in the knowledge that all the correct steps and procedures have been taken at the right time and in the right way.

Key elements in a credit control system

GETTING TO KNOW YOUR CUSTOMER

Any credit manager worth his or her salt will tell you that the collection of cash owed to any business does not begin after invoices have been rendered, or indeed after invoices have become overdue for payment. The management of credit begins at the precise moment when your customer asks you to deliver your goods or provide your services in advance of payment. Although it has become common practice for commercial operations in the United Kingdom to allow a period of credit, usually around 30 days from the date of invoicing or delivery, there is no legal obligation at all to do so and any business can quite properly insist that every one of its customers pays in cash in one form or another at or before supply. That, after all, is what the retail sector does with most of its daily transactions.

The giving of credit has developed to such an extent in this country, however, that to refuse to do so is likely to cause commercial difficulty and to lose you sales. How then can you deal on equal terms with your competitors while at the same time avoiding the risk and costs involved in late or non-payment of your invoices?

Part of the answer is to acknowledge the cost of providing credit as described in Chapter 1 and to incorporate those costs into your pricing structures. If you can estimate, for example, that your invoices are paid on average after forty-five days, then by incorporating into the price of your goods or services an interest element to include the rate of interest that your bank charges you for that amount for one and a half months, you will be covering the cost of that delay in payment. In addition, however, and to ensure that you are dealing with customers who can pay when required, or who are in a position to support the kind of credit facility which will be required to cover the volumes of products or services they are ordering, it is equally important to have some basic information to hand about that customer and his or her ability to pay.

Some of that information about your existing customers may be available to you already from your own internal sources. Your sales or marketing departments may already be aware of your customers' buying habits and whether they are likely to order large amounts in bulk every few months, or are more likely to buy smaller volumes on a weekly basis. Similarly, your accounts department will have information at its disposal to confirm the paying patterns adopted by particular customers. They can identify those customers who pay promptly in accordance with agreed contractual terms and those who stretch things to the very last minute until you threaten to sue or to terminate supplies.

If, however, you do not have that basic information at your disposal or if you are dealing with a new customer applying for a line of credit, then it is vital that you begin the credit management process at the earliest possible date by asking those customers for the basic information you will need in order to assess whether the risk you are taking in providing them with credit is commercially worthwhile. In doing so you may be changing your habit from the automatic provision of credit to customers unknown to you, to a position where you are actually inviting your customers to apply to you for a credit facility, the implication being that unless the basic information you require is provided, that credit will not be available. Trade credit should be applied for and properly assessed, not given automatically as of right. Moreover, continuous monitoring is vital in assessing your established customers' ongoing ability to pay.

Form 1 sets out in the form of an application for credit facility the basic information you will need for your decision-making process. You will note that it distinguishes at the outset between a company, a sole trader and a partnership but that in each case the information sought relates to the principal protagonists, whether they be directors or proprietors, and ensures that full trading addresses and telephone numbers are obtained. The personal addresses of sole traders and members of partnerships should also be sought to enable you to check for County Court Judgments and perhaps the local Electoral Roll for verification of the information received.

In addition, details as to the nature of the business and its date of commencement are sought to help you to decide whether the applicant is in a market sector which you consider to be one of high or low risk and to give you an indication of how long he or she has survived in that sector!

Full details of the applicant's banking arrangements should be obtained, together with the customer's consent to your seeking references on his/her business, primarily so that a banker's reference can be sought as well as the trade references which are listed, but also for future reference in the event of a default when you may wish through your own bank to update the creditworthiness of your customer by requesting bank-to-bank confirmation of resources available.

The enquiries relating to trade premises are principally designed to give comfort as to the stability of the applicant, as is the request for copies of the last three years' trading accounts, which should preferably be audited and if appropriate filed with the Registrar of Companies within the time limits imposed by the Companies Acts. If your applicant is unable or unwilling to provide those accounts then again you have a good but negative indication as to his or her past trading history.

It is also advisable to ask for copies of any charges or guarantees which have been given to secure or support the company's existing borrowings. Usually, you will be supplying your goods or services as an unsecured creditor and therefore if any charges have been created by your customer over specific property, such as the business premises or particular machinery or equipment, or if a floating charge has been granted over its assets generally, then this will mean that the value of the business's assets to be realised and distributed to creditors on a receivership or liquidation may be seriously reduced.

A sheet of the applicant's notepaper will also be useful, partly to indicate the professionalism of the potential customer but also to provide an opportunity to double-check the basic information sought, such as the names of partners, the

Form 1 Application for a credit facility

Items in this box are for office use only

Date Received ☐

New Account ☐ Change of Address ☐ Close Account ☐ Change of Title ☐

To be completed by [Customer] [Supplier/Sales Representative].

Full Legal Title ______________________________

Sole Trader ☐ Partnership ☐ Limited Company or plc ☐ Co. Reg. No. ☐

Delivery Address

Name ______________________________

Street ______________________________

Town ______________________________

County ______________________________

Postcode ______________ Telephone No. ______________________________

Statement Address (If same as delivery address, please state so)

Name ______________________________

Street ______________________________

Town ______________________________

County ______________________________

Postcode ______________ Telephone No. ______________________________

Business Activity (please specify) ______________________________

Method of Payment: Cheque ☐ Direct Debit ☐ BACS ☐ Other ☐

If other please specify: ______________________________

Form 1 **continued**

(To be completed by Customer)

Application for a credit facility (page 2)

I/We request you to open a Credit Account in the name of:

____

With a Proposed Credit Limit of: ______________ per month.

Trade References

I/We authorise you to take up references from the undermentioned bank and trade sources:

1. Name ______________ Account No. ______________
   Full Address ______________

2. Name ______________ Account No. ______________
   Full Address ______________

3. Name ______________ Account No. ______________
   Full Address ______________

Bank Details

Name ______________

Address ______________

Sort Code No. ______________ Account No. ______________

Contact for Payment

Name ______________

Position ______________

Tel. No. ______________ Fax No. ______________

Form 1 continued

Details of Owner/Partners/Directors

I/we have read, understood and retained a copy of your conditions of sale (including the retention of title clause) and agree to trade in accordance with these for any goods supplied. We accept that title to all goods supplied to us will remain vested in [ ] Limited until all amounts outstanding from us on any account have been paid in full to [ ] Limited.

I/we also agree to comply with your settlement terms (specified within your conditions of sale).

I attach a sample of my/our headed paper to this form.

1. Name ____________________ Signature ____________________

   Home Address ____

   ____

   ____

2. Name ____________________ Signature ____________________

   Home Address ____

   ____

   ____

3. Name ____________________ Signature ____________________

   Home Address ____

   ____

   ____

Form 1 continued

Customer Visit Report
(To be completed by Supplier/Sales Representative.)

(This report should contain key information about a prospective new customer, i.e. length of time in business, size of business, where they have previously purchased goods from, financial information, etc.)

____
____
____
____
____
____
____
____
____
____
____
____
____
____
____
____
____
____
____
____

Signature ______________________________ Date __________

Signature ______________________________ Date __________
(Regional Manager)

identity of directors, the registered office of a company, the company's registered number and its trading address.

It is also useful to obtain some idea from the customer as to the amount of monthly credit facility which he or she feels is required. The figure inserted may give rise to unbridled mirth in your credit department but it may also give you some indication as to the volumes of purchases which are anticipated. If they are sufficiently high, then they may encourage you to negotiate with your customer some alternative and more secure method of payment, for example by confirmed letter of credit or accepted bill of exchange.

The certificate required by the applicant is an important part of this document. It confirms that the information provided is accurate and that it is intended to induce you to provide the credit facility sought. This immediately creates a special relationship between you and your applicant, since not only will your customer be liable to pay you for goods ordered under the credit facility arranged, but also he or she is making a clear statement about the information provided and the intention in providing it. If it turns out that any material facts were false and that you relied upon them in agreeing the credit facility, then a misrepresentation will have arisen which may entitle you to unwind any contract entered into or claim damages in lieu for any consequential loss arising. This might give rise to a claim separate from your straightforward money claim for goods supplied and delivered.

Finally, it should be noted that the applicant's certificate gives specific authority to take up bank and trade references, which can be important as banks will no longer give references without the signed consent of their customers. It also acknowledges receipt of a copy of your company's conditions of sale, confirms the applicant's agreement to trade in accordance with those conditions without exception and asserts your retention of title rights over your goods until all outstanding amounts due from your customer have been paid in full. We will come to the importance of the establishment and enforcement of conditions of sale in a later chapter.

APPLYING FOR REFERENCES

Trade references

Once you have received your credit application from your potential customer it is important that the information you have obtained is used properly and not simply filed away without further consideration. Trade references should be taken up and **Letter 1** is in a form which is designed to elicit a prompt response providing specific information about your customer's trading history.

It has to be accepted that the trade references which are supplied by your customer are likely to be suppliers with whom he or she is on reasonable terms at least. In such cases a simple enquiry as to whether that customer is a good person to do business with is likely to receive a favourable response, perhaps sub-

Letter 1

Letter applying for trade reference

Dear [name] [avoid Sir/Madam]

[ ] Limited

Will you help us please? Your customer above wishes to open a credit account with us and has informed us that we may ask you for a reference to confirm their credit integrity. We need to know the following:

How long have you traded with them?

What is the amount of credit (value) you allow them?

What payment terms (period) do you allow them?

Are payments to these terms: (please tick)

- prompt?
- up to 2 weeks overdue?
- up to 4 weeks overdue?
- more than 4 weeks overdue?

Have you ever had to stop supplies or take third party or court action against them?

If ever we can help you with trade references we will be delighted to do so.

Yours sincerely

Credit Manager

P.S. For speed you may fax, e-mail or telephone your reply. Please keep the stamp inside the SAE for the cost of the call.

ject to a paragraph excluding liability for any claims or losses which may arise as a result of that representation. Such a reply is of little or no use whatsoever!

It is much better to be clear and specific about the credit facility which your customer has sought and to ask a number of precise questions to which the referee can quite easily supply precise answers. It is important to know how long the customer has been known to the referee, the amount of credit facility normally allowed, the terms of trading (that is to say, 30 days, 60 days or longer) and whether your customer is in the habit of paying promptly in accordance with these terms or not. The answers which are given will enable you to assess the views of other suppliers within the customer's trade and to judge how far you can reasonably go to satisfy your customer's request for credit and the likely effect the cost of that credit will have on your profit margins.

Letter 2 Letter applying for bank reference

The Manager
[The Supplier's Bank] plc
Address

Dear Manager [preferably name]

Application for a bank reference

[ ] require credit facilities from us and have given us written signed authority (see attached) to seek a credit reference from their bankers. They are:

[Name of Customer's Bank] plc
Address
Sort code
Account number

Please will you give your opinion whether [ ] is creditworthy for the amount of £ [total amount of credit] against payment terms of 30 days from date of invoice.

Will you also confirm if a fixed or floating charge is held against any of the assets of the company.

Thank you

Your sincerely

Credit Manager

On occasion, you may be applying for a trade reference to a supplier with whom you may be in competition. While you may have to view the replies you receive in the light of the supplier's attitude to your application, you may also wish to omit some of the information you are giving in your letter, such as the amount of credit facility which is being considered.

While a full response to a written application will provide you with the basic information you are seeking, quite often the referees concerned will be far more frank and forthcoming if the references are taken up by telephone. Their tendency may well be to give you information on the applicant's creditworthiness and upon his or her current trading position more freely over the telephone rather than going into print and to provide some anecdotal information, market rumour or just good old-fashioned gossip which may be valuable. In that event, **Letter 1** can be used as a checklist of specimen questions with which you can break the ice with the referee and try to obtain some further, and perhaps more illuminating, information about your prospective customer.

Bank references

Apart from the advantage that information about your customer's bank accounts gives you in the event that you are trying to locate funds against which you can enforce a judgment (by way of garnishee proceedings) should you have to sue at a later stage, it is entirely appropriate that you should take up banker's references when starting a trading relationship and **Letter 2** provides an appropriate form for your application.

It should be noted that the application for a bank reference and more particularly the interpretation of the reply requires some degree of skill. As in the case of trade references it is also easy to get back an answer which is not explicit and therefore worthless to you. On the other hand, if you are clear about the credit line which is being sought and the payment terms which are being proposed then the enquiry whether your customer is 'good for such a facility' should elicit a more meaningful response.

Even so, you may need to recognise some of the codes which are used by bankers when replying, such as:

'Undoubted for your figures'	– the highest rating possible
'Respectable and good for your figures'	– a good risk worth taking
'Customer not known to us for long'	– your applicant has recently switched banks – find out why
'Capital fully employed'	– a danger warning
'We cannot speak for your figures'	– think again!

In addition, you should also be aware that some bankers are reluctant to provide references direct to applicants and will only respond to another banker. For that reason you should as a matter of courtesy mention that the referee should feel free to reply to your own bank if preferred.

OBTAINING A CREDIT STATUS REPORT

As a form of additional comfort and in order to back up the basic information you have already sought from your customer and his or her trade and bank referees, it is often wise to seek confirmation of that information from an independent source and perhaps also to seek additional financial information about your customer's business and general creditworthiness.

Although you can do this yourself in the case of a company by applying for an up-to-date search of the Companies' Register, which will give you some further insight about the directors and shareholders of the company, its share capital structure, its latest accounts and the existence of any charges or debentures on the company register, and while you can check to see whether there are any County Court Judgments registered against your customer, there are now many specialised credit reference agencies providing this information at very short notice or even on-line, together with further analysis in relation to the company's recent commercial performance and an assessment of their credit rating.

The information provided will enable you to ensure that there is no confusion about the correct corporate or proprietorial name of the business with which you are about to trade. This is an elementary point but one which can often cause confusion if, for example, your sales representatives and accounts department think they are dealing with a partnership called ABC & Co. whereas they are actually dealing with a company known as ABC Limited. In the latter case the liability of shareholders will be limited to the amount of the share capital in the company, whereas the liabilities of the partners of ABC & Co. would be joint and several for the full amount of the debt without limit. Your risk assessment in each case is likely to be considerably different as a result. The accuracy of the name of the business is also essential should it ultimately become necessary to take legal action. Issuing a claim against the wrong trading style (name) can be costly and embarrassing.

For similar reasons it is important for you to identify if you can the full names and addresses of all proprietors and directors, the location of all branches and depots where the business is carried out and more particularly where the company's assets are held. You also want to have details of charges, debentures, County Court Judgments, turnover, net profit and net asset value, which will all add to the ammunition you require to make a decision. Finally, the agency will provide its own assessment of your customer's creditworthiness, which will provide you with additional guidance.

Further information about credit reference agencies, including a list of the larger organisations, is available from:

The Institute of Credit Management
The Water Mill
Station Road
South Luffenham
Oakham
Leics LE15 8NB

RISK ASSESSMENT

On receipt of all the details you require you will be in a position to make an informed decision as to your potential customer's creditworthiness. As your business expands and your customer base grows you may not have time to reach specific decisions in individual cases. It may be easier to categorise your customers according to your assessment of the risk to which your business is exposed by extending credit facilities to customers in a particular range of business or of a certain size. Risk categorisation should not of course be confused with the credit rating which you give to your customer. Because of the frequency of orders received and the pattern of sales to an individual 'blue chip' company you may wish to impose a credit limit of, say, £5,000 to ensure that your invoices for sporadic purchases are not left outstanding for too long. In that case, however, you may wish to place that particular customer in a 'no risk' category so that you spend very little time checking his or her payment records and reviewing the limits you have set.

On the other hand, in the case of a small company which orders your goods or services regularly, a £5,000 credit limit may amount to a very 'high risk' which you would like to keep an eye on far more regularly. This will enable you to review that customer's position, the frequency of orders, the volumes involved and the timing of payments to you. Your assessment will include whether the business generated as a result of the credit facility is sufficient to justify the risk involved.

In between these two extremes will lie your normal customer base, and if you are engaged in dealing with a business in which you have a substantial number of accounts which have to be checked repeatedly to ensure proper supervision of the collection process, you will find that the categorisation of risks will do a great deal to reduce the workload of your credit managers. This is achieved for the following reasons:

1. You will be able to concentrate your resources upon the appraisal and reappraisal of your 'high risk' customers.
2. By concentrating your efforts you will be able to ensure that your 'high risk' customers perform strictly within the terms you have agreed with them.
3. With the benefit of your experience you may be able to move 'high risk' customers into an 'average risk' category as a result of profitable trading with them, and if you see measured and properly financed growth within their business.
4. Ultimately, you will obtain a substantial and reliable base of customers with whom you have built up strong trading experience ensuring the maximisation of profits and the avoidance of bad debts and write-offs.

When dealing with your 'high risk' customers you should ensure that appropriate security for payment is obtained by adopting one of the methods advocated in Chapter 6. Alternatively, you could insist upon cash with order, or at the very least the agreement of your customer to a shorter credit period, but these issues will be dealt with later.

Applying the credit limits agreed

CONFIRMING TERMS OF CREDIT

Once you have made your decision and on the assumption that a credit facility is to be offered to your customer, it is important that the terms upon which you are agreeing are confirmed in writing. If the facility is not specifically confirmed and you simply begin trading with your customer, then the implication may arise that you have acceded to the request for credit set out in his or her application and that that is the basis of the contractual relationship between you.

Letter 3 sets out an appropriate letter in which, having acknowledged receipt of your customer's application, you are in fact offering specific credit terms

Letter 3

Letter confirming credit facility

Dear

May I introduce myself. I am [Sally Jones, the Credit Services Manager].

You will be pleased to know that we have now opened a credit account for your company, account number [123456]. My sales colleagues may have already contacted you about this but we too in Credit Services would like to thank you for your business.

To ease communication and to provide prompt service, [John Smith] in this department will be responsible for your account. He can be contacted on his direct line which is [number]. The credit terms applicable to your account are:

Payment terms :30 days from date of invoice
Credit limit :£3,000

Our other terms are as set out in our Conditions of Sale (copy attached). We strive to keep costs to a minimum to ensure that we can offer our customers keen prices and excellent service. To do this prompt payment is important. If your payment is not received by the due date you will be contacted. If the delay is caused by a problem of our own making please contact us and we will resolve it quickly.

You may also be contacted if your credit limit is exceeded. If you need to increase your credit limit we will be glad to review it.

Please confirm your acceptance of these terms by signing one copy of this letter below and returning it to me in the stamped addressed envelope provided.

Yours sincerely

Credit Services Manager

I hereby acknowledge and accept the credit facility described above and that your Conditions of Sale will apply exclusively to all dealings between our companies.

Signature ....Date ....

Duly authorised for and on behalf of

[ ] Ltd

which require his or her acceptance. It is a condition of that acceptance that the customer accepts the extent of the credit limit you have imposed. Although this is often treated as an internal matter and the credit limit is not always disclosed to a customer, the express agreement of that limit in advance can be a valuable tool if at some future date you consider the customer's position has become vulnerable or if you feel you would prefer to have the benefit of an express written agreement to support your position. It is vital that your customer also accepts that your trading relationship will from that time forward be governed by your conditions of sale.

Once your proposal has been formally acknowledged and accepted by your customer, then your future trading relationship will be established. As we will see shortly, the rights and obligations of each party will have been defined in your contractual terms and it will then be up to the managers of your business to decide how the rights created are to be enforced, in what manner, at what frequency and how severely. Those decisions will depend to a considerable extent on the degree to which your managers have recognised the importance of cash to the business, the cost of providing extended or prolonged credit terms and to what extent they recognise the difficulties which will arise if they allow their customers to pay invoices properly due as and when they see fit. On the assumption, however, that the lessons covered by previous chapters have been properly acknowledged we can now go on to look at how your contractual rights and obligations can be accurately determined and enforced.

APPLYING YOUR CONDITIONS OF TRADING

Document 1 at the end of the chapter (see p. 48) sets out a framework for conditions of sale. They are designed principally to protect the seller's rights, to limit potential liabilities and to provide some degree of security for the recovery of the debt which the buyer will owe following the supply of goods or services.

The basis of the sale should be set out specifying that the goods will be supplied in accordance with the seller's quotation or the buyer's order, subject to the seller's acceptance of that order but in either case subject exclusively to these conditions of sale. The object is to shut out the ability of the buyer to impose his or her own terms on the transaction. The authority of the seller's employees or agents is defined and restricted, as is their ability to advise or make recommendations to the buyer. Firm emphasis is placed upon the requirement for written acknowledgments or written confirmation from the seller specifically in relation to any additions to, or variations of, the agreement before those additions or variations can be enforceable.

Similarly, it is sensible to emphasise the need for written confirmation of any order submitted by the buyer and place responsibility strictly on the buyer for ensuring the accuracy of the terms of that order. If goods are to be manufactured by a process specified by the buyer, then he or she must indemnify the seller in respect of any losses arising for breach of any intellectual property rights arising from that specification, and in any event the seller reserves the right to make changes in that specification to comply with any safety or other statutory requirements. The right to cancel is subject to the seller's specific agreement in advance and an indemnity from the buyer in respect of all losses arising.

The provisions relating to the price of the goods and terms for payment should include the seller's right to increase the price of goods on notice.

The seller is entitled to send his or her invoice at any time after delivery or if the buyer wrongfully fails to take delivery of the goods, and payment becomes due without deduction (save for any discretionary discount) within 30 days from the date of the invoice. The time for payment should be expressed within a contract, so that any default on the part of the buyer will entitle the seller to terminate the contract and claim damages for repudiatory breach of contract by the buyer. The alternative rights open to the seller include the right to charge interest on all overdue accounts until payment, usually at a rate of around 3 per cent or 4 per cent over the base lending rate of the seller's bank or perhaps 1.5 per cent per month. It should be appreciated that, although it is preferable to provide for contractual late payment interest, since the enactment of the Late Payment of Commercial Debts (Interest) Act 1998, there may be available a statutory right to interest on late paid commercial debt. The legislation is being introduced in three stages:

- for the first two years – 1 November 1998 to 31 October 2000 – small businesses will be able to claim interest from large businesses and the public sector on debts incurred under contracts agreed after that date;
- the right to claim interest will be extended, from 1 November 2000 to 31 October 2002, so that small businesses will also be able to claim from other small businesses on debts incurred under contracts agreed after that date;
- from 1 November 2002, all businesses and the public sector will be able to claim interest from all businesses and the public sector on debts incurred under contracts agreed after that date.

These dates are those that have been proposed by the government. However, the Act does allow the government to amend the phasing arrangements if the desired improvements in payment culture have not come about. The government will publicise these changes widely as they happen.

The current (1999) statutory rate of interest is 8 per cent above the base rate. Businesses cannot contract out of this legislation but, of course, when drafting in the rate for contractual interest, the statutory rate ought to be compared.

The vital areas of any contract for the supply of goods include delivery, risk and title. The point at which risk in the goods passes (that is to say, the time when liability for the loss of the goods will arise) and therefore the point in time when the prudent businessman or woman will insure those goods, is at actual delivery or at the point in time when the goods become available for delivery to or collection by the buyer.

The fact that title (i.e. ownership) in the same goods may pass at a later time often causes confusion, but again the retention of title by the seller is designed to provide a form of security for him or her should the buyer default in payment. The provision under these terms is that ownership of the goods will not pass to the buyer until the seller has received in cash the full price of the goods and any other goods for which payment may then be due. Until that time the buyer holds the goods on trust for the seller and undertakes to keep them stored separately from other goods in the buyer's possession. While the buyer is entitled to sell those goods, he or she is obliged to account to the seller for the proceeds of sale and to keep those proceeds separate from the buyer's other funds. Until the goods are paid for, the seller reserves the right to repossess the goods and to enter into any premises where the goods are stored in order to do so.

Such an 'all monies' retention of title clause is a very powerful tool which an otherwise ordinary unsecured creditor can use to his or her advantage, especially where the buyer has gone into insolvency. If the retention of title clause has been properly incorporated into the sale contract and provided that the seller can clearly identify his or her goods, then such goods will not form part of the assets of the buyer. Therefore, in an insolvency situation, secured creditors of the buyer, especially holders of a fixed and floating charge contained in bank debentures, will not be able to get their hands on the seller's goods. Despite challenges from such unsecured creditors and insolvency practitioners determined to uphold the *pari passu* rule, 'all monies' clauses have been upheld by the English courts. It must be appreciated, however, that in relation to manufactured goods, mixed goods and proceeds of sale, any attempt to benefit from a retention of title clause is likely to be struck down by the courts as amounting to an unregistered charge on the goods or the resale proceeds. Such benefit can only be *granted* by the buyer to the seller and not *retained* by the seller. Retention of title is a complex and changing area of the law and therefore, like your general terms of trading, should be tailor-made as far as possible to your business and industry. Specialist advice is therefore recommended.

The terms should also specify what happens in the event of the insolvency of the customer. In certain circumstances, if a voluntary arrangement is made between the buyer and his or her creditors, or if a receiver or administrator is appointed under the Insolvency Act 1986, then if the customer is a company which is continuing in existence until being formally wound up, a current contract between the parties may still exist leaving outstanding obligations on the part of the supplier. In such circumstances, however, or in the event that the buyer ceases business or seems likely to become insolvent, the seller is entitled to terminate the contract, to suspend further deliveries and to pursue such remedies as he or she may have (including the enforcement of a retention of title clause or demands for payment due) against the buyer.

It should always be appreciated, however, that the preparation of contractual terms, and in particular those which apply to specialised areas of trading, does require a significant degree of legal expertise. Unless such expertise is sought and followed there are real risks that a supplier and purchaser, when entering into a contract for the supply of goods or services, will quite innocently find and fall into the many pitfalls which abound.

While it may not be practical or cost-effective to take legal advice before supplying each of your individual customers, it is certainly advisable that you should take the advice of a solicitor or your in-house legal department, if you have one, when the terms of your standard conditions of sale are being negotiated (*see* **Document 1**), or if any of your customers insist upon amendments or variations to those conditions before placing an order with you. Although this may involve you in an initial cost which may seem expensive at the time, over a given period that cost will invariably save time, effort and further expense in the future by avoiding uncertainty and creating legal obligations which both you and your customer clearly understand.

Doc. 1

Conditions of sale

For the reasons set out in italic above, it is important for all businesses to engage a specailist solicitor to draw up Conditions of Sale specifically for their own circumstances. Areas to cover might include:

Definitions (e.g. 'buyer', 'seller')
Quality
Price
Quotations
Delivery/date/arrangements
Passing of property and risk to buyer/retention of title
Terms of payment
Time limit for raising disputes
Right to interest
Loss or damage in transit
Acceptance of goods
Variations to contract
Patent rights/indemnity
Force majeure
Jurisdiction/applicable law
Assignment and subletting of contract
Right to progress and inspect goods
Warranties and liability
Severability
Insolvency and bankruptcy

Using your sales documentation

IMPOSING YOUR TERMS

Having considered carefully the conditions of sale which you feel are most appropriate to your business and which are likely to balance the need to provide you with sufficient ammunition to take forceful action against delinquent debtors, while at the same time avoiding your loyal and prompt-paying customers running to their lawyers every time they wish to place an order, the next consideration is the best means by which to have those conditions applied to your day-to-day contracts.

Although your contract or terms of sale provide that the seller's conditions shall govern the contract to the exclusion of any other terms, that provision will only be effective if it forms part of the contract with your customer. If the earliest point at which your customer sees your conditions of sale are on the back of your invoice and that invoice is dispatched after the delivery of your goods, then your conditions are worth less than the paper they are printed on because the contract and terms upon which it is based will already be in place.

The point here is that the terms which apply to a contract for the sale of goods are those which are agreed between the parties at the moment in time when agreement to sell and to buy is reached. In *John Snow & Co. Ltd* v. *DBG Woodcroft*, Justice Boreham said: 'To entitle a party to rely upon a particular term, he must prove that the terms were brought to the notice of the party sought to be bound before, or at the time that the contract was made.' If, therefore, a seller provides a quotation which incorporates his or her conditions of sale and that is accepted by the customer without further comment, then the seller's conditions will apply to the contract because the buyer will be deemed to have accepted those conditions when he or she accepted the quotation.

On the other hand, if in response to the quotation the buyer submits a written order which incorporates the buyer's own terms of purchase and the seller then supplies on the basis of that order, the implication will be that the seller has accepted the buyer's terms without further amendment. The only way the seller can avoid that implication is by using a suitable clause in his or her conditions of sale. By sending back to the buyer an order acknowledgment form, again referring to the original conditions of sale, the seller can thus override the buyer's terms and reimpose his or her own.

This form of contractual table tennis, commonly known as 'the battle of the forms', can be extremely frustrating and quite often can only be circumvented either by one party submitting to the will of the other, or by some form of negotiation and compromise taking place. All too often, however, the parties to the contract, having submitted their own terms to the 'exclusion' of any others, carry on on the assumption that their terms will apply, which leads inevitably in the event of a dispute to argument, delay and another unpaid invoice!

The only solution to this quandary is to ensure that on all your sales documentation, namely your quotations, estimates, specifications, order acknowledgments and delivery notes, clear emphasis is placed on the fact that supply of goods or services is being effected on your contractual terms.

Letters 4 and 5 provide sample forms of quotation and estimate, the difference being that while a quotation confirms a fixed and predetermined price for the goods or services offered, an estimate is exactly what it says, namely an estimate of the amount to be charged, subject to a reasonable variation up to the date an invoice is delivered. Each form emphasises the following points in particular:

1 That the letter does not amount to a formal offer which is capable of immediate acceptance by the buyer. The reason for this is that upon such acceptance the contract would be in place and while that might be attractive from your sales department's point of view, you may wish to have the opportunity to consider, for example, the terms of your customer's application for credit, or you may wish, depending on the timing of the order which is placed, to vary some of the provisions in your proposal with regard to price or delivery.

2 That the quotation or estimate is submitted, and any subsequent contract is intended to be subject exclusively to your conditions of sale, the advantage being that your customer's attention is drawn immediately to those conditions, to the terms for payment and to the fact, for example, that title is to be retained until payment is effected in full. Unless your customer opens negotiations immediately to vary those terms you will at least be in a position to make the point that the terms upon which you are dealing have been known from the outset, and at best your customer may have accepted the quotation and your conditions without comment.

Letter 4

Form of quotation

Dear [name]

We are pleased to set out below the terms of our Quotation for the supply of [ ]. We must emphasise that this Quotation is not a tender document and as a result any Order which is placed by you will be subject to formal acceptance confirmed by an appropriate Order Acknowledgment. We also confirm that this Quotation and any subsequent contract entered into will be subject exclusively to our Conditions of Sale, a copy of which is printed on the reverse side of this document.

Quantity	Description	Price	VAT

This Quotation will remain open for a period of 4 weeks from the date of this Quotation and delivery will be effected approximately 4 weeks after the date on our Order Acknowledgment.

Yours sincerely

Letter 5 Form of estimate

Dear [name]

We are pleased to set out below the terms of our Estimate of the price to be charged for the supply of [ ]. We should emphasise that this Estimate is not a tender document and as a result any Order which is placed by you will be subject to our formal acceptance confirmed by an appropriate Order Acknowledgment. We also confirm that this Estimate and any subsequent contract entered into will be subject exclusively to our Conditions of Sale, a copy of which is printed on the reverse side of this document.

Quantity Description Price VAT

This Estimate will remain open for a period of 4 weeks from the date of this Estimate and delivery will be effected approximately 4 weeks after the date on our Order Acknowledgment.

Yours sincerely

3 It is always wise to limit the 'life' of a quotation or estimate for a reasonable period. This will not only encourage the customer to make his or her decision within that time-scale but it will also give you an element of control on your pricings and other terms of business if an order is not placed within the relevant period.

Letter 6 is the type of order form you are likely to receive from your customer confirming not only the quantities which he or she wishes to order and the price the customer wishes to pay but also confirming that the order is placed subject to his or her terms of purchase. As already indicated, if you then supply on the basis of that order, then unless some form of compromise takes place and the results of your negotiations are properly recorded in writing, the implication will be that you have supplied in accordance with your customer's terms, which would probably omit any specific date for payment, any right to claim interest on overdue accounts and would certainly not include any right to retain title in the goods pending payment.

Letter 6 Order form

Dear [name]

Order No.

We thank you for your Quotation/Estimate dated [ ] and are pleased to confirm our order for the following goods in accordance with our terms of purchase which are printed overleaf.

Quantity Description Price

Yours sincerely

The only effective counter to this form of order is to stick to your guns and to send back an order acknowledgment in the terms set out in **Letter 7**. While that letter acknowledges and accepts the order, it re-emphasises that such acceptance is subject exclusively to your conditions of sale, which again gives the opportunity for your customer to come back to you to negotiate a compromise before delivery. If the customer fails to do so, the implication will again be that your conditions have been accepted and your customer's terms have been abandoned. That implication will be reinforced in particular if further reference is made on your delivery notes or on any consignment documents, bills of lading or the like to the fact that your conditions are the ones which apply to the contract, and if you can get these final documents signed by your customer or his or her employees when delivery actually takes place.

Letter 7

Order acknowledgment form

Dear [name]

We write to acknowledge and confirm our acceptance of your Order No. [ ] which is accepted subject exclusively to our Conditions of Sale, a copy of which is printed on the reverse side of this document. We would advise that delivery will take place on or about [ ].

Yours sincerely

Finally, in order to make your contract documents work it is always useful to ensure that your invoice sets out in detail all the relevant information which your customer will need to pass it for payment promptly to the bought ledger department and which will enable them to post the transaction accurately in their records. **Form 2** sets out the basic requirements of such an invoice including the date, the references of both parties to the transaction, your customer's order number, his or her account number with you, details of the transaction and the total amount due. As a last reminder you should always repeat that payment is due within 30 days from the invoice date. As mentioned already, there is no point at this stage once the contract has been effected in trying to refer again to your contractual terms, which by that time will already have been determined by the outcome of 'the battle of the forms'.

Form 2 Invoice

TEL NO.	
FAX NO.	
FOR ENQUIRIES ABOUT INVOICES, TEL:	

CUSTOMER NAME	
CUSTOMER A/C NO.	
BRANCH NO.	
ORDER TYPE	

INVOICE ADDRESS

GOODS DELIVERED TO

ORDER NO.	ORDER DATE
DELIVERY NO.	DELIVERY DATE
INVOICE NO.	INVOICE DATE

PRODUCT CODE	DESCRIPTION	SIZE	QUANTITY	UNIT OF CHARGE	NET PRICE	VALUE EX VAT	VAT RATE

TOTAL EXCL. VAT	
VAT	
TOTAL PAYABLE £	

PAYMENT TERMS: PAYMENT TO BE RECEIVED NO LATER THAN 30 DAYS FROM DATE OF INVOICE

CONTACT FOR QUERIES

Please retain invoice for six years for VAT requirements

Issued in conjunction with the Company's Terms and Conditions
Registered Office:
Registered in England number 222222
VAT registration number 222222

OBTAINING SECURITY FOR PAYMENT

A supplier's conditions of sale are intended to create a series of rights and remedies which will enable prompt action to be taken against a customer who is in default. They are designed to compensate the supplier for the losses which arise on late payment, for example by allowing interest to be charged. If it is felt by the supplier that even those protections are insufficient to secure his or her position properly with a particular customer, some additional comfort may be obtained by seeking some other form of security which will give additional rights in the event of late payment or default. We have already looked at the powers which an appropriate retention of title clause can give to a supplier, namely the right to recover goods which are not paid for and which can be positively identified as being goods supplied by the supplier. To some extent, however, the supplier's ability to enforce those rights depends upon whether or not his or her customer has obeyed the rules.

If, for example, the customer has not stored the supplier's goods separately or kept them properly identified as being separate from his or her own, or if the customer has carried out work to the goods or merged them with his or her own goods to form a new combined product, or has simply sold the goods and paid the proceeds into a bank account, then it is quite likely that a receiver or liquidator could successfully challenge the retention of title rights which are being claimed. Further, as explained above, such rights may already have been lost as a matter of law.

Guarantees

The only other practical method of protection is to seek some form of guarantee from a third party who agrees to indemnify the seller in the event that the buyer fails to perform his/her part of the sale contract. That assurance may be obtained in the case of a company from another company within the same group or from the company's directors by taking from them a guarantee to secure future payments.

To some extent guarantees are an exception to the usual rule under English law that a contract can be made orally. In this country guarantees must be in writing and they must describe clearly and precisely the obligations of the guarantor. **Letters 8** and **9** set out appropriate letters from a holding company or subsidiary in the same group as the customer, or alternatively from one or more directors of the company itself. The following are the main points to be recognised in such guarantees:

1 That the consideration being provided by the supplier for the guarantee is the continued supply of goods to the customer.
2 That the guarantor not only provides a surety for the customer's liabilities but also undertakes to indemnify the supplier on demand.

Letter 8 Letter of guarantee from holding company or subsidiary*

Dear Sir or Madam

We are the holding company/subsidiary of [ ] Limited which has applied to you for a credit facility in the sum of £10,000.00 per month. We are pleased to confirm that in consideration of your supplying [ ] Limited we hereby guarantee all liabilities of [ ] Limited to your company howsoever arising and undertake to indemnify you upon demand without set-off or deduction in respect of all losses, claims, damages, costs and any other form of indebtedness to you by [ ] Limited which may arise.

This guarantee is a continuing security and primary obligation which shall not be affected by any waiver, release or indulgence allowed to [ ] Limited.

Yours faithfully

**Such a letter has two prerequisites*:

- *a board minute authorising a director or the company secretary to sign it;*
- *the power to give such a guarantee in the memorandum and articles of association.*

Letter 9 Letter of guarantee from a director of the company

Dear Sir or Madam

I am writing to you as a director of [ ] Limited and I am pleased to confirm that in consideration of your supplying [ ] Limited I hereby guarantee all liabilities of [ ] Limited to your company howsoever arising and undertake to indemnify you upon demand without set-off or deduction in respect of all losses, claims, damages, costs and any other form of indebtedness to you by [ ] Limited which may arise.

This guarantee is a continuing security and primary obligation which shall not be affected by any waiver, release or indulgence allowed to [ ] Limited.

Yours faithfully

3 That the liability will be discharged without any set-off, deduction or other form of contra accounting, even though the supplier may be liable under some other contract to the guarantor or the customer direct.

In addition, the guarantee is expressed to be a continuing security, which means that even if the customer's liability under the contract is reduced to zero, the guarantor's liability will arise again should further debit balances accrue. Finally, the guarantee is expressed to be a primary obligation so that the supplier is not obliged to exhaust all his or her rights and remedies against the customer before applying to the guarantor for payment. Even if the supplier waives any rights against the customer or allows time to pay, that would not affect the supplier's rights to enforce his or her claims directly and without delay against the guarantor.

Bills of exchange

An alternative method of providing security for payment is for the customer to provide his or her supplier with a bill of exchange, which unlike a cheque is an unconditional order to pay. The security is provided when the bill is 'accepted' by the customer's bank, raising an obligation on that bank to meet the bill when it becomes due.

There are three parties to an 'accepted' bill. The supplier will prepare the bill and deliver it to his or her customer. The customer will then pass the bill to his or her bank, who accepts it by writing 'Accepted' across the face of the document and adding a signature, thus confirming that the customer is in funds or has a facility sufficient to pay the amount shown. This endorsement confirms the customer's bank's undertaking to honour the bill when presented.

Once this security is provided, the bill, which is a negotiable instrument, can then be sold on or 'discounted', thus providing funds for the supplier at a date earlier than the due date for payment. The discounted bill will have deducted from its face value an interest and facility charge. To obtain full value the supplier must obviously wait until the due date for payment by the drawee before presenting the bill to the accepting bank, which will be obliged to meet the amount of the bill in full.

EXPORT SALES

Clearly, when a supplier is involved in export sales different considerations will apply. Retention of title clauses will prove much more difficult if not impossible to enforce and the guarantees of foreign holding companies or directors resident abroad will be of much less immediate value because of the delays and expense inevitably involved in taking legal proceedings outside the United Kingdom.

In these circumstances, alternative methods of payment must be found and one answer may be the presentation of a foreign bill of exchange drawn by the supplier and accepted by his customer. As with UK bills, a sight draft is payable on demand while a term draft requires payment at a specified future date or dates following a specific event such as delivery, but in either case the exporter will use a collecting bank to act on his or her behalf to assist in the enforcement of the bill.

The supplier will prepare the draft bill and send it to the customer's bank for acceptance while a standard form of mandate is sent by the supplier to his or her

Form 3

Example of a sight bill of exchange

Reproduced by kind permission of NatWest

	24 March 1997	***£100,000***
On	***Sight***	for the value received, pay against the bill of exchange
to the order of	***British Success Story (Exports) Limited***	the sum of
	One Hundred Thousand Pounds	
effective payment to be made in	***Sterling***	without deduction for
and free of any taxes, import, levies or duties present or future of any nature.		
Drawn on	***A.N. Other Co. Ltd***	
	Overseas	***P.P. British Success Story (Exports) Ltd.***
		Director

bank giving instructions as to how the collection of the bill is to be dealt with.

Some foreign bills of exchange may have export documents and conditions attached so that the supplier can deal with delivery and the receipt of payment by instalments. When a customer is considered to be creditworthy and has a track record of prompt payment, a 'clean' bill of exchange may be delivered without such conditions attached. Otherwise the instructions to the supplier's bank will cover areas such as how charges are to be dealt with, how the proceeds of sale are to be transmitted back to the supplier and any other information that is to be of use in the course of collection. Standard forms of bills of exchange and instructions to bank are provided by most banks, but examples are set out in **Forms** 3 and 4.

Letters of credit

Circumstances may arise when a bill of exchange, even when properly prepared and presented by the banking system, will still provide the supplier with insufficient security for an export to a high-risk customer or even to a good customer

Form 4

Standard instructions to collecting bank

Reproduced by kind permission of NatWest

NatWest
Outward Bills
PO Box No75, 38 Colmore Circus
Birmingham B4 6DJ
United Kingdom

Telephone 0121-234 2000
Telex 885361 NWBLDN G
Swift code NWBK GB 2LB

Customer ID

1 Send documents abroad by
Courier Yes/No
Customer ref:

Collecting Bank (Buyer's Bank)

2

Date

Please deal with the enclosed in accordance with instructions marked [X]

3

	Bills of Lading	Bill of exch	State-ments	Sets of in-voices	Certs of origin	Insce Cert/ policy	Pack list	Cert of Ship/Sea Waybill	Air waybills	Postal receipt	Non neg B/L	Other documents
Enclosed	of											

Whereabouts of any missing original Bills of Lading

4 Deliver documents against:
- [ ] Payment
- [ ] Acceptance and return of draft
- [ ] Acceptance
- [ ] Special instructions (see below)
- [ ] Acceptance/payment may be deferred until arrival of goods

Charges: 5

	NWB	Agents
Drawee	[ ]	[ ]
Principal	[ ]	[ ]

Charges may [ ] may not [ ] be waived

Cable advice 6
- [ ] Dishonour charges Principal
- [ ] Proceeds charges Principal
- [ ] Proceeds/Dishonour charges Principal
- [ ] Proceeds charges drawee
- [ ] Proceeds/Dishonour charges drawee

Amount and currency

Insurance covered by Principal [ ] drawee [ ]

7
Protest for: [ ] Non-acceptance [ ] Non-payment
No Protest for: [ ] Non-acceptance [ ] Non-payment

Special instructions

NWB Use Only

In **case of need** refer to/for information our local agent is
- [ ] Who will co-operate in obtaining payment
- [ ] Whose instructions may be followed unconditionally

Settlement Instructions * delete as appropriate and complete all details in appropriate section

1 Proceeds and/or* **Charges** should be passed to **Sterling** Account No ___/________
held at ________ Branch/Bank Sort Code

2 Proceeds in the full/the amount of* ________ should be credited to
Currency Account No ___/________ in ________ (Currency Name)
held at ________ Branch/Bank Sort Code

Charges should be debited to my Sterling Account shown in section 1 [ ] Currency Account shown in section 2 [ ]

Remit proceeds at my expense to my account by Urgent Transfer [ ] Bankers Payment [ ] Chaps [ ]

Forward contract details Amount ________ Rate ________ Reference ________ Date ________

Please contact for instructions
Name (s) ________
Company name and address ________

Telephone number ________ Facsimile number ________

Signature of customer ________

NWB1860 Rev Nov 95-1 we agree with the terms and conditions overleaf

Complete only if advance required
Advance the face value/the sum of ________
Now [ ] Other [ ] ________

Branch Sanction (Bank use only)
Authorised by ________

Rate of interest ________ % fixed/variable

Acknowledgement

Name ________

Company name and address ________

We NatWest acknowledge receipt of documents as specified
Amount ________
Your Reference ________
When corresponding please quote:
our reference ________

For and on behalf of Outward Bills

who happens to be in a country where the banking system is suspect. One way around this particular problem is to require payment by letter of credit which can be expressed as an 'irrevocable' authority to pay (**Letter 10**), that letter being an instruction to the customer's bank to make certain payments to the supplier in full once a number of conditions are satisfied.

If there are doubts about the banking system in the customer's country, then the supplier can insist that the letter of credit is confirmed by a 'blue chip' bank in another jurisdiction, or, for example, one of the clearing banks in the United

Letter 10

Confirmed irrevocable letter of credit

To: [Supplier]
[Address]

We have been requested by [the buyer's bank] to advise the issue of their irrevocable Credit Number [ ] in your favour for account of [the buyer] of [address] for £10,000 (SAY TEN THOUSAND POUNDS STERLING) available by your drafts on us at .... sight accompanied by the following documents namely:

1 Signed invoices in triplicate certifying goods are in accordance with Order Number [ ] dated [ ] between [the buyer] and [the supplier].
2 Marine and War Risk Insurance Certificate covering 'All risks' warehouse to warehouse, for 10% above the CIF value, evidencing that claims are payable in [buyer's country].
3 Complete set 3/3 Shipping Company's clean 'on board' ocean Bills of Lading made out to order of the shippers and endorsed to order of [the buyer's bank] marked 'Freight Paid' and 'Notify [the buyer] of [address]'.

Covering: Mechanical Spare Parts CIF [the buyer's place for delivery]
Shipped from UK Port to [the buyer's place for delivery]
Partshipment prohibited Transhipment prohibited
Documents must be presented for payment within 15 days from the date of shipment.

We are requested to add our confirmation to this Credit and we hereby undertake to pay you the face amount of your drafts drawn within its terms provided such drafts bear the number and date of the Credit and that the Letter of Credit and all amendments thereto are attached.

The Credit is subject to Uniform Customs and Practice for Documentary Credits (1993 Revision), International Chamber of Commerce Publication No. 500.

Drafts shown under this Credit must be presented to us for Payment / Negotiation / Acceptance not later than [ ]
and marked 'Drawn under Credit Number [ ] of [the buyer's bank]'

Dated..
Signed ....
[the confirming bank]

Form 5 Bill of lading

Shipper		BILL OF LADING	B L No.
			Reference No.
Consignee			
Notify address			
Pre-carriage by*	Place of receipt by pre-carrier*		
Vessel	Port of loading		
Port of discharge	Place of delivery by on-carrier*		

Marks and Nos	Number and kind of packages	Description of goods	Gross weight	Measurement

Particulars furnished by the Merchant

Freight details, charges etc	SHIPPED on board in apparent good order and condition, weight, measure, marks, numbers, quality, contents and value unknown, for carriage to the Port of Discharge or so near thereunto as the Vessel may safely get and lie always afloat, to be delivered in the like good order and condition at the aforesaid Port unto Consignees or their Assigns, they paying freight as indicated to the left plus other charges incurred in accordance with the provisions contained in this Bill of Lading. In accepting this Bill of Lading the Merchant expressly accepts and agrees to all its stipulations on both pages, whether written, printed, stamped or otherwise incorporated, as fully as if they were all signed by the Merchant. One original Bill of Lading must be surrendered duly endorsed in exchange for the goods or delivery order. IN WITNESS whereof the Master of the said Vessel has signed the number of original Bills of Lading stated below, all of this tenor and date, one of which being accomplished, the others to stand void.
Daily demurrage rate (additional Clause A)	

*Applicable only when document used as a Through Bill of Lading	Freight payable at	Place and date of issue
	Number of original Bs.L	Signature

Kingdom. Such a 'confirmed irrevocable' letter of credit will give the supplier good security for his or her exports, provided of course that he or she lives up to the conditions which are attached to the letter itself. These will usually consist of conditions relating to delivery, certification as to country of origin, the provision of certain documents of title such as bills of lading (**Form 5**) and of course the quality of the goods themselves.

The procedure adopted is that the customer arranges for the letter to be 'opened' with his or her bank and confirmed if necessary by the confirming bank. The letter should set out the conditions which the supplier has agreed to and which must occur before payment is effected. As in the case of bills of exchange these will relate to the timing of the delivery, the confirmation of title or ownership of the relevant goods and certain other formal confirmations which may be required. Needless to say, the confirming bank must ensure that all conditions attached to the letter are complied with in every detail before payment is made. For that reason it is vital for the supplier to ensure that he or she pays very close attention indeed to the procedures required in opening the letter of credit and in complying with its conditions. A checklist dealing with the main points is set out at **Document 2**.

It should also be noted that as in the case of bills of exchange, letters of credit can provide a source of finance for the exporter by discounting and selling on the rights attached to the letter. The buyer then holds the letter until maturity before presenting it to the original party liable under the bill or letter of credit for payment. This system, known as forfaiting, will require the endorsement or confirmation of the negotiable instrument by a bank which is acceptable to the forfaiting market. Any endorsement must be unconditional and irrevocable, and provided these conditions are complied with the exporter will be able to discount his or her bills and letters of credit and receive full value less the amount of discount charges which are applied, without having to wait for the bill of exchange or letter of credit to mature.

Credit insurance

The provision of credit to commercial customers, whether in domestic or export markets, inevitably carries a degree of risk. Even long-established trading partners can suffer a reversal of fortune and, if a customer should become insolvent, the resulting bad debts can seriously affect the supplier's cashflow and potentially threaten its own solvency.

However, there is a well-established method by which a supplier can secure protection from the effects of a buyer's insolvency or protracted failure to pay. Credit insurance from a specialist underwriter can provide indemnity against the non-payment of invoices, typically ensuring payment of around 80 per cent of the value of an insured debt. The cost of the premiums can simply be built into the price of the goods or services supplied.

Doc. 2 Letter of credit checklist

1 Ensure that the buyer when arranging the letter of credit with his or her bank, understands the main points to be included. Ideally, the supplier should supply the buyer with a list of conditions relating to delivery dates, shipment details and expiry dates for inclusion in the letter of credit to ensure that misunderstandings are avoided.
2 The supplier should ask for sight of the buyer's bank's usual form of letter of credit to ensure that it meets all requirements and to double-check that all the points of information which the bank will wish to include have been agreed with the buyer.
3 If the letter of credit is to be confirmed, for example by a UK bank, that UK bank will notify that confirmation to the supplier and as soon as the confirming letter is received it should be checked thoroughly to ensure that all the conditions attached to the contract which are of relevance in relation to the acceptance of the credit are included and are entirely accurate.
4 If for any reason any of the details on the letter of credit are inaccurate, then the buyer, the issuing bank and the confirming bank should be contacted immediately to ensure that an amended letter of credit is prepared as a matter of urgency.
5 The supplier should ensure that any letters of credit, confirmed or otherwise, received by the business are delivered to a single person or department. That person should then distribute copies of the letter and require immediate confirmation from all departments (marketing, production, sales and despatch as well as the credit control team) that the conditions attached to the letter of credit which relate to their activities can be performed by them without delay.
6 Finally, before acceptance the letter of credit should be checked again to confirm that the following areas are in all respects accurate and in accordance with the contract:
   (a) that the basis of pricing including terms of delivery (for example CIF or FOB) are set out;
   (b) that a sufficient period of time is allowed before expiry of the letter of credit to allow for shipment by the supplier;
   (c) a full and accurate description of the goods is included which should be repeated word for word on the supplier's invoices;
   (d) that an appropriate method of payment is specified, for example 'in sterling at sight in London';
   (e) that the method of delivery of the goods is specified as agreed;
   (f) that the documents listed in the letter of credit to be provided as a condition of payment are in the form agreed and available.
7 Having shipped the goods and prepared the documentation, the supplier should now present the documents as quickly as possible to the confirming bank.
8 In making the application the supplier should, when sending the request for payment to the confirming bank:
   (a) include a list of the documents enclosed, confirming that they comply with the documents required by the letter of credit;
   (b) set out clearly the confirming bank's letter of credit reference;
   (c) check to ensure that the documents enclosed comply exactly with the terms of the letter of credit specification;
   (d) check to ensure that those documents contain all relevant shipping and letter of credit references so that they conform to each other;
   (e) check to ensure that the relevant dates for delivery and particularly for expiry of the letter of credit have been complied with;
   (f) indicate the method by which the supplier wishes to receive payment, for example by cheque, draft or a credit at his or her own bank.

Although credit insurance has been available in the UK for around eighty years, the market is still growing steadily. Underwriters today offer a range of policies to meet different needs, including cover for a company's whole turnover if required. Other policies may cover a company's key customers, or accounts in excess of a specified value with the supplier being responsible for losses up to that threshold, or a series of transactions with a specific customer over a fixed period of time, or even a single high-value sale.

In recent years, the value of export credit insurance has grown substantially as more companies seek to expand sales in new and possibly volatile markets overseas. Exporters can obtain cover both for commercial risks and for exposure to a variety of political hazards, with indemnity against currency convertibility problems and the recognised 'insured perils' of contract frustration, contract cancellation, export restriction and import restriction. Moreover, it is now possible to arrange cover for UK and export commercial risks and export political risks within a single, easy-to-administer policy.

As with bills of exchange and letters of credit, an export credit insurance policy can be used to provide the exporter with trade finance facilities. The policy is endorsed with the effect of making the bank a joint policyholder, and the bank can be linked to the insurer's electronic policy management system to reduce administration effort and streamline the approval of advances. Both domestic and export credit insurance policies are written subject to certain terms and conditions, compliance with which is essential to ensure prompt payment in the event of a claim. These can vary between insurers, but typically include:

- the restriction of cover to trade invoices only;
- the exclusion of intra-group sales;
- the requirement to provide evidence of a buyer's protracted default (i.e. non-payment after a specified maximum extension period beyond the due date) or insolvency (i.e. the business is adjudicated bankrupt or is the subject of liquidation, administration or receivership proceedings under the Insolvency Act 1986 or its equivalent abroad).

Other conditions may be attached to the policy. These will most likely relate to the internal credit management procedures of the insured, typically concerning:

- the length of credit to be granted;
- requirements for assessing the creditworthiness of customers;
- the setting of credit limits for each buyer;
- cash collection timings and procedures.

The obtaining of credit insurance may, therefore, impose disciplines that promote a more effective credit management system within a business.

In addition to its 'defensive' role in credit management and cashflow protection, credit insurance should also be viewed positively as a sales expansion tool. The insurer's extensive information database that forms the basis for underwriting decisions can assist a policyholder in targeting good quality sales leads while avoiding poorer risks.

To summarise, the potential benefits of commercial credit insurance include:

- protection against the consequences of a UK or export customer's unforeseen insolvency or protracted late payment;
- indemnity against both foreign commercial and political risks;
- the ability to use a credit insurance policy for raising trade finance;
- enhancement of a company's overall credit management function;
- improved sales targeting.

In conclusion, credit insurance can enable a company to trade with confidence.

Creating and maintaining an efficient system

So, now that the management of your organisation has recognised the real cost of a delayed or inconsistent flow of cash into the business and has recognised the key elements involved in any system which is to be geared towards the consistent collection of cash due and owing, what are the first steps to be taken towards the creation of efficient cash collection procedures? The basic requirement may be the provision of a system which:

1 coordinates the efforts of the various divisions within your organisation;
2 fulfils your customers' expectations and requirements;
3 leads towards a 'collection philosophy' which becomes well known to all your employees as well as to your customers and suppliers.

Once such a system is established an efficient and business-like reputation will be attained within your market which in itself will make the collection of cash significantly easier.

A COORDINATED SYSTEM

We have already considered the disadvantages faced by the kind of company which sets too great a store by a consistent drive for turnover while ignoring or at least relegating to a position of minor influence the need to convert its sales into hard cash. If those disadvantages are to be overcome then it is important that everyone in the organisation should be made aware of the priorities which have been decided upon by the senior management of the company and the role of each individual in that company in achieving those priorities.

We have also seen that in most organisations the general philosophy of the business is almost always provided by its leaders and so it is important that that leadership gives a clear indication of its intentions at the earliest opportunity. The easiest way to do this is to lead by example and to emphasise the need for the prompt collection of balances due to the company and the avoidance at all costs of any opportunity which would allow your customers to delay that process.

Clear evidence of the seriousness of your intent should be given within the structure of your organisation. Your credit managers should no longer be treated as 'debt collectors' only and should be given clear lines of responsibility and accountability for the tasks allotted to them. They (and never the sales managers) should be given responsibility for deciding credit limits and terms of payment for individual customers but they should also be given appropriate training and information to ensure that they are properly equipped for the task.

In addition, your credit managers should be directly responsible for obtaining payments from customers within the terms agreed.

The combined effect of the responsibility, training and information will increase the status of the credit manager and provided he or she is given appropriate access to the senior management of the company – perhaps being directly accountable to the finance director or the managing director of the business – his or her influence upon that company's liquidity and ultimate profitability will grow. A useful starting-point may be provided by **Letter 11**, which

Letter 11

Memo to production, marketing, sales and collections staff

How we are going to increase sales, improve profits and speed cash flow through effective credit management

Profitability starts at the time of the sale, continues with excellent service, products, and administration and is reinforced through effective credit management. Cash flow permeates every nook and cranny of the business – we are all responsible. There are three areas under our review of financial systems that are going to improve cash flow and profits greatly.

Communication
Many disputes arise between our customers, our marketing/sales people and our financial services departments because of lack of clarity and openness about procedures. Just as we explain to our customers in a positive way our prices, products, quality, delivery and service, we need our sales/marketing people to explain our credit terms to customers with the same conviction; it is all part of the deal. Your support is also needed to uphold these when customers stray from them. A new accounts application form, approved by Marketing, has been designed and our marketing literature is going to include details of our credit facilities.

Eliminate own goals
There is no better excuse for a customer not to pay a bill on time than problems of our own making. Customers should not have to pay for inefficiency. Since the costs of these self-made errors are not included in our prices they reduce our profits significantly. They also damage goodwill with our customers which can lose us sales. A fall in sales has a disproportionate effect on profitability and is very damaging to our business. New procedures and forms will be in place soon to improve the speed at which we clear customer queries. The best way to reduce paperwork is not to make the mistake in the first place.

Credit Services
Disciplined and sometimes unorthodox credit management practices help reduce the costs associated with slow payers and bad debts. Despite the need to persuade customers to conform to our terms of business we are going to try to achieve this in a more positive way, hence 'Credit Services' and not 'Credit Control'. We are trying to 'sell' the idea to customers to pay on time, hence the new credit application form, change in style of our letters to customers, and training to improve our dealings with customers by telephone.
No one ever went out of business because of effective credit management combined with excellent products and services, dynamic selling and creative marketing. Let's get it right. I need to count on your support. Thank you.

Finance Director

is an initial memorandum from a person in a position of senior management within the company to his production, marketing, sales and collection staff. Although the style of each company will differ, this note is designed to cover the main areas which should concern any company following a review of its internal system. The memorandum should endeavour to encourage communication between departments, emphasise the importance of exchange of information, confirm the status of the credit manager and the role it is intended he or she should play within the corporate structure, and finally give notice that further discussion and explanation will be given and that feedback from all relevant staff is invited.

To ensure that all credit managers understand their duties and responsibilities, they should also have the benefit of a detailed job specification setting out the principal tasks and the reporting procedures required. A sample form of such a job specification is set out at **Document 3**.

Doc. 3

The commercial credit manager: job specification

Objective

To protect the overall quality of the Debtor Asset. To maintain the highest possible volume of Debtors (Sales) for the shortest possible time (Collections) and so to minimise the erosion of profits deriving from overdue accounts. To keep bad debts to a minimum commensurate with the risk inherent in the attainment of the Company's sales targets.

Responsibilities

He/She will:

1 In liaison with Sales Management, Financial Management and Purchasing Management prepare for the approval of the Board a company credit policy including standard payment terms for use in the company's conditions of sale and take the initiative in proposing such amendments to the standard payment terms as he/she feels appropriate.
2 Prepare annually for approval of the Board a realistic budget analysed over such company divisions as may be decided upon for debtors expressed in days of credit sales outstanding or on whatever other formula is agreed. Submit in liaison with Sales Management any adjustments to the debtors budget as may derive from any proposed sales promotion schemes or special marketing efforts.
3 Prepare at intervals agreed with Financial Management a forecast of cash collections analysed over sales division or department based upon the budgeted days of credit sales outstanding adjusted by the current financial and sales ledger conditions.
4 Negotiate a contract with an agency for the provision of credit information, where appropriate.
5 Obtain on each customer sufficient information as to permit him/her to decide upon the level of investment prudent for each such customer by way of trade credit (the investment level) bearing in mind the financial condition and management skills of the customer and the company's

Doc. 3 **continued**

sales/profit ambitions in that customer. Place each account in a 'risk category' to a standard formula and ensure that both investment level and risk category are recorded on the account, the customer file and the data bank.

6 Maintain a constant monitor and review the investment levels every six months with the object of increasing them in the light of good account experience and/or improvement in the customer's financial condition in order that the generation of increased sales on each account is, as far as is prudent, not impeded for lack of an adequate credit line.

7 Open a credit account on standard payment terms for any proposed new customer, meeting his/her creditworthiness standards and, where he/she so considers prudent, authorise a departure from standard terms if essential to meet the sales objective. Make customers aware of standard terms and conditions and any amendments which will apply.

8 Negotiate and decide the individual payment terms and investment levels for each overseas customer in the light of the customer's creditworthiness and the overall economic/political conditions in the relevant export market.

9 With the help of credit insurance brokers, consider the desirability for credit insurance on all or part of the budgeted debtor exposure.

10 Implement a system whereby all goods/services to be supplied on any one account are monitored against the investment level before execution of each order.

11 Implement a system in liaison with all affected parties, including systems analysts, for the proper recording of all transactions with each customer on a sales ledger account. Ensure that each account is updated regularly (preferably daily). The sales ledger system at all times shall provide an analysis of the unpaid balance on each account over the individual outstanding items.

12 Maintain and control a query system to ensure that problems are resolved promptly and accurately.

13 Ensure the regular and prompt submission of invoices to each customer and a monthly statement of account to all customers. Monitor the balance on each account with a proper system of follow-up procedures towards the collection of the unpaid balance at the due date.

14 In liaison with the Sales Management, decide when and for how long supplies of goods/services should be withheld from persistently overdue accounts.

15 To institute such collection action or legal proceedings as are necessary on these accounts.

16 Protect the company's interests by ensuring company attendance at meetings of creditors which involve any customer in insolvency proceedings.

17 Make and monitor claims in insolvency proceedings.

18 Monitor retention of title claims.

19 Liaise with credit insurance underwriters/brokers to ensure that maximum recovery is achieved.

20 Provide the Accountant with details of any VAT bad debt relief claim, and any recovery thereof.

Doc. 3 **continued**

21 Supply monthly to the Board, Sales and Finance Management a report on debtors based on an aged debtor analysis, to include a comparison of collection performance to target, any variances to be covered by explanatory notes. If so required, the monthly debtors report shall be analysed over sales divisions or market outlets and include an aged debtor analysis of major customers showing for each customer the actual days of credit taken compared with sales terms.
22 Calculate, in conjunction with the Accountant, the provision required in the accounts to cover the risk of bad and doubtful debtors and to have any bad debts which are to be written off approved by the financial director or chief accountant.
23 Prepare annually for approval by the Board a financial budget for the credit control department including recommended staff levels, provision of cars, cost of status enquiries, credit insurance, training, bank charges, computer time and any capital expenditure required for new machines and furniture, etc.
24 Establish and maintain a procedures manual.
25 Supervise and manage the credit department in accordance with the departmental budget, ensure that the credit department is adequately staffed and that the responsibilities in each job grade are properly defined.
26 Prioritise and schedule the work flow of the credit department.
27 Set collection targets for credit department staff, or geographical regions, where appropriate, to ensure that all customers pay their accounts within the agreed payment period.
28 Monitor the performance of each member of the credit department.
29 Interview and select credit department staff.
30 Ensure the further training and development of all members of the credit department.
31 Maintain and encourage good customer relations at all levels through personal contact and visits.
32 Keep him/herself up to date with modern credit management practice and the development of new and relevant data processing systems, by reading, attendance at seminars and active participation in the affairs of the relevant institutions.
33 Keep him/herself up to date with insolvency procedures and associated matters including VAT bad debt relief, retention of title, etc.
34 Take all steps considered necessary to ensure that the credit control function is executed at all times in the best interests of the company.
35 Establish links with other Credit Managers in same trade and industry credit groups, if company policy permits.
36 In accordance with company policy, refer problem debts to a collection agency or solicitor.

Attributes required

While not necessarily an accountant, he/she will have a sufficient knowledge of accountancy to enable him/her to implement the company's accounting and budgeting practices. He/she will have sufficient understanding of accounts analysis to allow a proper interpretation of a set of accounts in

Doc. 3 **continued**

terms of the assessment of the credit risk in conjunction with other customer information available. He/she will have an understanding of mercantile and company law as it applies to all aspects of trade debtors including the legal processes of debt collection.

If responsible for export debtors, he/she will have adequate knowledge of credit insurance (home and export), country risk, factoring, direct debit, the discount and money markets, etc. to allow him/her to advise on such matters when necessary. He/she must be computer literate.

Preferably a member of the Institute of Credit Management he/she will be of pleasant disposition, and act as a sales orientated ambassador for the company, capable of conducting financial negotiations both in-house and with customers at all levels.

Responsibility line
As a member of the company's senior executive, the credit manager will normally be managerially and functionally responsible to the financial director.

One of your short-term aims to assist the credit manager in the fulfilment of his or her duties will be to use the system of cooperation and coordination that you have created to obtain and to record properly all the information which your organisation currently has concerning your customer, in so far as that information relates to the way that customer pays your invoices. For example:

1 Your credit managers will have retained the basic information provided by the customer when applying for a credit facility as set out in **Form 1**.
2 Your sales department will have a good idea who the decision makers are within your customer's business and should be able to find out quite easily which of the directors is likely to have authority to sign cheques and how many signatures are required.
3 Your despatch department may have additional information at its disposal concerning other locations or addresses to which goods are delivered to your customer.
4 Your accounts department should be able to give you some information about your customer's current payment procedures including who receives incoming invoices to whom they are passed, who clears them for payment, who deals with the preparation of cheques and how the signing process is dealt with.

Once collected, all of this information should be retained in the kind of customer history record sheet which is set out in **Forms 6(a)** and **6(b)**. This form can be retained either in hard copy or adapted for use in a computerised system, but basically the main ingredients will be the same. Provided the information is

Form 6(a) Customer history record sheet (manual version)

Customer Tel. No.:	Customer Name:	Managing Director:	Customer:
Customer Contact:	Customer Address:	Finance Director: Cheque signatories:	Debtor No.: Credit Limit: Terms: Cheque run date:

Date	Name	Remarks

Form 6(b) Customer history record sheet (adapted for computer screen)

Customer Details

Customer Name		Debtor Number	
Customer Address		Customer Contact	
		Customer Supervisor	
		Financial Director	
	(Postcode)	Managing Director/Owner	
Telephone			
Fax			
Account Handler		Credit Limit	
Revenue Executive		Payment Terms	
		Category	
Company History			
Special Payment Terms			
Discounts Agreed			

Contact History

Date	Amount	Month	Comments/Agreed Actions	Promise	F/U Date

updated regularly your company will be able to keep a constant check upon the trading patterns and payment habits of your customer, as well as keeping a reasonably close eye on their business, so that if you do have to enforce your contractual rights you will have a pretty good idea where they are operating, where their senior directors can be found and where their assets in the form of plant, equipment, stock and property, perhaps including your own supplies, are kept.

FULFILLING YOUR CUSTOMERS' EXPECTATIONS

It almost goes without saying that the most essential members of your credit management team are your customers! Without them even the most efficiently coordinated system is doomed to failure. It is therefore important to ensure that good customers are not driven away by an inflexible or inefficient system, and to ensure that your customers are persuaded to be as helpful and as supportive as possible in your collection efforts.

Because your credit management team is dealing with your customers at particularly sensitive times, in particular when they are applying for credit and when you are asking them for payment, a sensible approach designed to get your customers on your side is to develop considerable loyalty on their part which will contribute substantially to your company's marketing and sales efforts. Again, part of the coordinated approach which is advocated above and the contribution your credit team can make to marketing and sales must be emphasised to everyone involved in those processes.

How then can customer loyalty be increased? The heading of this section gives something of a clue. It is inevitable that customers become most frustrated and disenchanted with a company's supplies or services if performance does not match up to their expectations. This can happen either because they are 'over-sold' or if circumstances change in a way which affects the supplier's ability to perform as promised. 'Over-selling' should be avoided at all costs.

Of course, if your company is likely to deliver on time and in accordance with the terms of your contract then it is satisfying to be able to write to confirm the position. **Letter 12** does this, but at the same time politely reminds the buyer of his or her own obligations to be able to take delivery under the terms of your conditions of sale. The effect of this letter is therefore to put your buyer on notice as to your own intentions but at the same time providing some additional

Letter 12 Letter to customer confirming collection and delivery timescale

Dear Sir or Madam

We are pleased to confirm that our production and delivery arrangements relating to your Order No. [ ] are proceeding satisfactorily and delivery is likely to take place at the time estimated in our Order Acknowledgment dated [ ].

We are writing simply to ensure that your own arrangements for the acceptance of delivery are in place and to confirm that our invoice will be despatched to you at the time of shipment for payment under our Conditions of Sale.

If any of these arrangements is likely to cause you any difficulty, please let us know at once.

Yours faithfully

contact with you. This gives the buyer the feeling that you are providing extra service and a courtesy which perhaps he or she would not normally expect. It also provides documentary evidence that you have communicated the situation and have requested details of any likely 'difficulties'.

If, however, you find that for whatever reason the supply of your goods or services is likely to be delayed, then it is essential that your customer should be informed at the earliest opportunity. This is not simply to ensure that any notice required by your contractual arrangements should be complied with but also to give your customers the opportunity to rearrange their own position, for example by informing their own customers of the likely delay. Again, you are in effect building up and maintaining a dialogue with your customers which they will find of assistance in the organisation of their own businesses. **Letter 13** sets out the kind of letter that you should write as soon as possible identifying circumstances which may have arisen beyond your control which are likely to give rise to delay in delivery. The letter refers to your conditions of sale allowing an appropriate extension of time in such circumstances but confirming that you will be making every effort to find alternative sources of supply or means of delivery to enable you to comply with your contractual arrangements at the earliest opportunity.

Letter 13 Letter to customer explaining production difficulties

Dear Sir or Madam

We refer to your Order No. [ ] which was confirmed by our Order Acknowledgment dated [ ]. You will recall that delivery was due to take place on or about [ ] but we regret to inform you that due to circumstances beyond our control namely [the delay in delivery of raw materials] [industrial action taken by the employees of our suppliers] [default on the part of our carrier] it seems likely that [substantial] delay will arise in the delivery of your order to you.

You will recall that under the terms of our Conditions of Sale an appropriate extension in our time for delivery is allowed in such circumstances and we confirm that we are making every effort to find alternative sources of supply/carriage which will enable us to effect delivery at the earliest possible date.

It is inevitable, however, that some delay will arise. We will keep you informed as to our progress.

Yours faithfully

Letter 14 acknowledges that the delays have arisen as a result of circumstances which are within your control but specifies them clearly and provides your customer with a new delivery schedule upon which he or she can rely. In normal circumstances, provision of this information is likely to gain you some sympathy from your customer, on the basis that every business suffers setbacks

Letter 14 Letter to customer explaining variations in delivery times

Dear Sir or Madam

We refer to your Order No. [ ] which was confirmed under the terms of our Order Acknowledgment dated [ ]. You will recall that our estimated time for delivery of these goods was [ ] but we are sorry to have to advise you that because of [production difficulties at our factory] [difficulties arising in the ability of our carrier to deliver to your premises] [amendments in your instructions with regard to delivery] there may be some variation and delay in the delivery schedule and the dates we originally estimated.

You may recall that under the terms of our Conditions of Sale the dates given for delivery were estimates only and were subject to variation on prior notice being given by us. In these circumstances, we are confident that the following revised schedule sets out a realistic basis for delivery of your order.

New Delivery Schedule

Date	Quantity	Description	Price	VAT

We hope that you will find these arrangements are in order but, if they present any difficulty, please do not hesitate to contact me.

Yours faithfully

of one kind or another from time to time. Once more, your customer would then be in a position to reschedule his or her own arrangements and to advise his or her own customers of the new times for delivery of your goods.

It is vital that if any of the information you are providing to your customer changes or further delay arises, then he or she should be informed at once. The letters you are sending should be reinforced by direct contact at the appropriate level by telephone or by subsequent meetings to emphasise the service you are providing and to build up a sense of communication between you, which, provided your timing is right, can only enhance the loyalty which will be built up between your organisations.

THE COLLECTION PHILOSOPHY

As with many other commercial decisions, the emphasis which is placed upon a company's collection processes will inevitably have to reach a level of compromise with a number of other factors. Sales still have to be maintained so it is not often feasible for the credit manager to use the sales force as a ready-made, on-the-spot, collection team. Similarly, if too much weight is put behind the collection process, if contractual terms become too onerous or credit limits are set too low and applied too rigidly, then customers will be driven away.

The balance which is struck and the way that your decision is communicated will determine the collection philosophy of your business and will be interpreted by your staff and customers accordingly.

Perhaps the safest way out of this dilemma is to adopt reasonable procedures that are commercially sound, that are generally accepted to be in accordance with good credit management practice and that you expect your own staff and your customers to comply with. In that way you are in a position to be seen as fair and efficient in your decision-making processes in so far as they relate to the establishment of credit limits and the setting up of terms of payment, while at the same time your staff and your customers recognise the importance which you place upon the strict compliance with your conditions of sale and, in particular, the time taken for your customers to pay invoices which are due.

Letter 15 Letter to customer on credit review

Dear

Better service to you

You have been a customer of ours for some time now. Thank you for your business.

Sales and marketing people are not the only ones who take customer service seriously; so do we in Credit Services. Account queries are both irritating and costly to both of us. This is why we have introduced procedures to reduce mistakes, and when they do occur, to clear them quickly. But we need your help.

The faster you can tell us of our mistake, the quicker we can resolve it. For any problem that affects your account with us, may I ask that you direct it to me personally. I guarantee that I will apply pressure in the right direction to get it resolved.

Our Conditions of Sale have also been changed (a copy is enclosed). These include new terms which make them fairer to prompt paying customers so that they do not subsidise slow or non-payers. They are:

- interest on overdue accounts;
- passing of risk and retention of title in goods supplied.

These are the terms on which we will be supplying all of our customers in future.

If ever you are unable to contact me direct, my colleague [name] will be pleased to help.

Yours sincerely

Credit Services Manager

Again, the most important factor in this process is the communication of information. **Letter 15** is designed to remind your customer of the existing trading relationship between you while at the same time giving notice that you have recently been reviewing your own internal credit systems. It goes on to advise your customer of the likely impact that review will have upon your relationship. The emphasis is upon the provision of an additional service by your company even though that service is designed specifically to avoid any reason for delay in the payment of your outstanding invoices. Further emphasis is placed upon the fact that you are trading under your conditions of sale and advising that those conditions have recently been updated to incorporate fresh terms which are likely to have some impact on your current trading practices.

Again, the emphasis is on communication and the door must always be left open for discussion and negotiation in relation to the terms that you wish to apply.

Provided that the changes you wish to impose are described promptly and fully to your customers and provided your credit terms are reasonable yet firmly imposed, you will quickly establish a reputation within your own market place for fairness and good service to customers who are loyal to you but firmness with customers who are not.

Building your own structure

How then can you adapt the lessons learned thus far into a credible and workable credit management structure for your own organisation? The starting-point, as for most management decisions, is to set out clearly defined objectives which your company and its staff can aim towards and then to hone the tools at your disposal to sufficient sharpness to ensure that these objectives can be achieved.

Of course, the objectives themselves will have to be measurable. The basic requirements, however, will be to minimise the financial risks to which you are exposed, to avoid bad debts, to increase your sales and to build up the best relations possible with your customers.

You should aim to use all the points we have discussed so far including the obtaining of information about your customer, the application of your conditions of sale, the use of your sales documentation, the obtaining of security for payment and the build-up of communication between your own divisions and with your customers to create the framework on which a custom-built credit management structure can be created for your own company.

We can now look in greater detail at the letters, forms and practices which may assist your organisation in that task.

A COMPREHENSIVE SYSTEM

For any system to be effective both your customers and your staff must understand it. Although there is a certain truth in the adage 'the sooner you ask the sooner you get paid' the timescales you set must also be reasonable if you are to avoid antagonising your customers and if you wish to build up the kind of loyalty we have discussed earlier. There is little point in allowing customers 30 day credit terms and then chasing them up ten days after you deliver your invoice. On the assumption, however, that the time for payment that you have set is accepted by your customers, there is no reason why you should not send them a statement of account on a regular basis (the frequency will depend on the volumes of sales involved) giving details of all the balances currently due to you.

A statement of this nature is set out in **Form 7** and the objectives of it are to ensure that your customers can match their data with yours, thus making it as easy as possible for them to authorise payment of the amounts listed. It is therefore vital to show your customers' names accurately, your account number and the date of the account together with full information referring to order numbers, invoice dates and balances due. The amount overdue should be highlighted in the most effective way possible and your customers should be encouraged to send back all or part of the statement with their payment so that you in turn find it easier to identify for which account the payment is destined.

If you find that in spite of sending statements your customer is still in default of your 30-day terms, action needs to be taken. You should follow whatever

Form 7

Statement of account and remittance advice

STATEMENT

DATE PAGE

ACCOUNT NUMBER

Name and address of customer

Name and address of supplier

The person responsible for your account is:

Tel:

Fax:

DATE	DOC. REF.	TRANS-ACTION TYPE	GOODS SUBJECT TO DISCOUNT	GOODS STRICTLY NET	TAX STRICTLY NET	TOTAL VALUE
					BALANCE DUE	
						- SETTLEMENT DISCOUNT - ALLOWED ONLY IF PAID BY DUE DATE

CURRENT	1 MONTH OLD	2 MONTHS OLD	3 MONTH & OLD

DATE PAGE

REMITTANCE ADVICE
Please detach and send with your remittance payable to:

Name and address of supplier:

ACCOUNT

DOCUMENT REF.	TRANS-ACTION TYPE	TOTAL VALUE	PLEASE TICK ALL ITEMS BEING PAID
SUBJECT TO DISCOUNT			BALANCE DUE
		- SETTLEMENT DISCOUNT - ALLOWED ONLY IF PAID BY DUE DATE	

collections procedure your company has established. Some firms use the telephone as the main means of collecting cash. This has been found to be by far the most effective method. It does, however, take time. You may therefore decide that only payment of invoices over a certain value should be chased by telephone, the remainder being sent a letter. The key to an effective collections system is to do whatever works for you. You may use one, two or three letters of reminder. You may use faxes, e-mail, personal visits or a combination. Experience will show what is most effective for your circumstances. And never forget, you want not only to get paid, but also to keep your customer happy.

Three possible first reminder letters are set out at **Letters 16(a), 16(b)** and **16(c)**. Your choice will depend on the circumstances and your personal preference. The key elements are that the letter is addressed specifically to the appropriate contact in your customer's bought ledger department who is responsible for ensuring that your invoices get paid. You should quote his or her name and reference, your account number, their order number, the balance currently due and the due date so your contact has all the information he or she needs. Your letter should refer to the terms of payment set out in your conditions of sale and you should remind him or her when those conditions were accepted, whether that was when credit facilities were applied for, when the order was placed, or when the order was acknowledged using your company's standard documentation.

Letter 16a Example of first reminder letter

Dear

Have you forgotten?

Your payment of £ [amount] for your [month] account has not yet been received. Is there a reason for this?

Please send your payment to reach us by [date].

Thank you.

Yours sincerely

Credit Services Manager

Amount overdue	:	£
Payment terms	:	X days from date of invoice
Credit limit	:	£
Account	:	123456

Letter 16b Example of first reminder letter

Dear

You generally pay your account promptly although lately I have noticed your payments, though regular, are consistently overdue. Is there any special reason for this? Extended credit is an overhead we both have to fight and of course prompt payment enables us to keep our costs down so that you benefit from competitive prices.

Will you please send your payment for [amount] today to enable us to continue to provide you with the prompt service you rightly expect from us.

Yours sincerely

Credit Services Manager

Amount overdue	:	£
Payment terms	:	X days from date of invoice
Credit limit	:	£
Account	:	123456

Letter 16c Example of first reminder letter

Dear

It's in the post!

If so, thank you. Will you please contact me with the details. If not, please send it today so that we receive it by [date].

Yours sincerely

Credit Services Manager

Amount overdue	:	£
Payment terms	:	X days from date of invoice
Credit limit	:	£
Account	:	123456

You should also make the point (which may be useful later if your invoices are subsequently disputed) that no query has by that time been raised with regard to the goods delivered or services rendered, or indeed in relation to the invoices which have been delivered. You should then indicate specifically and clearly what you wish the recipient of your letter to do. In this case you want your cash! You therefore make it perfectly clear that you wish to receive a cheque by return payable to your company. The signatory to the letter should be the credit manager responsible for the account, the same person who has written to the customer confirming the terms of your current trading relationship in the form set out in **Letter 15**.

In the case of new accounts with customers who have only recently agreed terms of trading with you and from whom you are perhaps seeking your first payment, it may be opportune to let your customer know that the agreed terms are to be applied strictly. A firm but friendly telephone call might well suffice. It is often worth telephoning just *before* payment is due to ensure that all is well, and that you can expect payment by the due date. If instead you decide to send a reminder letter, **Letter 17** provides a gentle reminder which, if delivered before the account becomes overdue, shows that you intend to start as you mean to go on.

ELIMINATING COMPLAINTS

Occasions may arise when customers will have cause to query your invoices or will complain about the standard of products delivered or services rendered. If that happens it is vital to ensure that you have in place a method by which that query is quickly acknowledged, investigated and replied to, so that delay in the payment of the outstanding invoice is avoided. The query may relate to the calculation of the invoice, or the fact that you have delivered only part of a consignment but have invoiced for the whole order, or it may even be a simple enquiry in response to your statement of account requesting a further copy of an invoice because the original has gone astray.

Whatever the reason for the query, the onus is firmly upon your company to resolve the problem fast. Otherwise the customer will feel perfectly justified in withholding payment of all or part of the relevant amount until your system gets itself sufficiently organised to respond to the point which has been raised.

The most efficient method of dealing with this situation is to set up an efficient query/complaints procedure. This will involve a system within your own organisation which ensures that each of your departments recognises the importance of their cooperation in providing a prompt response to any enquiry raised by a customer, no matter how trivial or how spurious that enquiry may seem. By using **Letter 11** you have already emphasised that point to your marketing, sales, production, despatch and collection departments. Now what you have to do is to ensure that your system works in practice. The starting point is a reply to a customer of the kind set out in **Letter 18**. This letter is personally

Letter 17 Reminder letter (new accounts)

Your Ref.
Account No.
Balance Due: £
Due Date:

Dear

I am writing to you following the delivery of goods/performance of services in accordance with your Order No. [ ] which was effected on [ ].

As you are aware from our Conditions of Sale which were accepted by you when you [applied for credit facilities] [placed your Order] [your Order was acknowledged] our terms for payment are thirty days net which following the delivery of our invoice on [ ] means that payment is due to us on [ ].

In the circumstances since you are a new account customer to us we would be grateful if you could ensure that you have everything necessary (for example appropriate approvals, cheque signatories and so on) to enable you to effect prompt payment on or before the due date.

I therefore look forward to receiving the balance due as shown above in accordance with our trading terms.

Yours sincerely

Credit Manager

addressed to the person raising the query, it sets out your account number and reminds your customer of the balance due. It refers specifically to a letter or telephone conversation on a particular date and provides a means by which the nature of that query can be recorded accurately.

As a commitment to the standard of service promised by the letter set out in **Letter 15**, your credit manager confirms that the relevant department has been contacted immediately to check the points which have been raised and provides his or her personal undertaking to come back to the customer within a specific timescale to resolve the position.

On the assumption that the query or complaint does not relate to the entire balance then due, your credit manager then reminds your customer that there is still a balance owing to your company which is not in any way connected with the queries which have been raised. The manager refers specifically to the relevant invoices or statements of account and then repeats his or her request for payment of the undisputed balance by return. The effect of this letter is therefore twofold. It gives the customer a sense of receiving an additional prompt and efficient service and at the same time it gives little or no leeway for delay or non-payment of balances which are properly due.

Letter 18 Letter to customer acknowledging query and requesting payment of undisputed part of debt

Dear

Thank you for bringing to my attention the queries concerning invoices [ ] and [ ]. These are now being dealt with and you will be contacted very soon with our findings.

Meanwhile, may I ask that you pay the undisputed part of the account which is now overdue amounting to £[ ]. Will you please send your payment to reach me by [date].

I have arranged that, from now on, my colleague [name] will contact you a week before the due date to discuss with you any outstanding queries so that these may be resolved quickly so avoiding overdue payment in future.

Yours sincerely

Credit Services Manager

Amount overdue	:	£
Payment terms	:	X days from date of invoice
Credit limit	:	£
Account	:	123456

As far as your internal procedures are concerned, **Letter 19** sets out a standard memorandum to the relevant department, giving full details of the customer, his or her account number, the relevant credit limit and the current balance due, requiring an immediate response to enable your credit manager to reply to the customer within the timescale he or she has promised. The customer query record sheet at **Form 8**, a copy of which is also sent to the department concerned, provides the same information but also gives details as to the exact nature of the query which has arisen, and the date it was received. It sets out the deadline by which a response must be given to the customer and leaves a space for the production, marketing, sales or despatch departments to give details of the remedial action which is to be taken to resolve the problem. When that form is returned by the relevant department to the credit manager, he or she is then in a position to reply to the customer's query or complaint either by negotiating some form of discount or allowance on the invoice delivered, or by delivering a letter as set out in **Letter 20** which again is addressed personally to the complainant. This letter quotes the relevant account number and the bal-

Letter 19

Query memorandum requiring response

Customer Name	Account No.	Credit Limit	Current Balance Due

I attach a copy of a query record sheet which gives details of a [letter] [telephone call] I have just received from [ ] which sets out in detail his [or her] reasons for delaying/refusing payment of our invoices.

You will see that in line with our company policy I have undertaken to get back to the customer within [24 hours] [2 days] and to enable me to do so I would be grateful if you could let me have by return, on the copy query record sheet provided, a note of the action you intend to take to respond to the query which has been raised and to resolve the position.

Regards

Credit Manager

ance due and then goes on to set out your company's version of events in a way which is designed to deal conclusively with the query raised.

Having put your case in a manner which is perfectly clear and leaves no room for your customer to doubt your company's position, you then go on in the second paragraph to confirm that under your conditions of sale the query raised does not justify any further delay for payment and requires your customer's cheque for the balance being withheld by return of post, again requesting payment direct to your credit manager so that any further delay or confusion can be avoided.

It is obvious that in establishing and maintaining the query/complaints procedure the cooperation of each division within the company is vital and this can only be obtained if the credit manager is given sufficient and sustained backing from his or her directors who must insist upon immediate compliance and replies to query memoranda. Without that support, delays in replies will creep in, the credit manager's authority will be diminished and your customers will again be allowed the kind of leeway which will build up your debtor lists and begin to impinge on the profitability of your business.

ISOLATING EXCUSES

Genuine queries or complaints always have to be dealt with promptly and effectively through your query/complaints procedure but occasions will arise when

Form 8

Customer query record sheet

Query
Reference Number: Received (date):
Recorded By:

Customer Information

Contact Name: Phone Number:

Contact Address: Credit Limit:

Current Balance Due:

Complaint Details

Details

Complaint Category:

Delivery Note Number:

Additional Information:

Number of Identical Queries: When?

Query Valid?

Invoice Number	*Invoice Values*	*Invoice Dates*

Corrective Action to be Taken

Signature ______________________________

Letter 20 Letter to customer responding to query

Dear

You will be pleased to know that credit note [number] for [value] has now been issued against invoice [number 1] for the overcharge and will be with you soon. Please accept our apologies. Concerning invoice [number 2] your buyer has been informed direct by our sales people that the charge is correct and consistent with our quotation.

Will you please now pay the undisputed part of invoice [number 1] and the whole of invoice [number 2]. Our Conditions of Sale (clause x), to which your company agreed, state that payment of undisputed invoices, or part, must not be withheld against those, or any proportion of those, that are in dispute.

Please now send your cheque for [amount] to reach me by [date].

Thank you.

Yours sincerely

Credit Services Manager

Amount overdue	:	£
Payment terms	:	X days from date of invoice
Credit limit	:	£
Account	:	123456

customers raise enquiries or respond to your demands for payment with replies which sound more like excuses than good reasons for delay.

You may believe that there are as many excuses for non-payment as there are orders or invoices, but generally speaking those excuses can be grouped into no more than half a dozen types which can be resolved, provided your credit managers are dealing with the situation firmly and positively. The essence is to ensure that the issues raised by the customer are narrowed as quickly as possible, that timescales for delay are shortened and strict deadlines are set for payment. It is also important to ensure that all conversations or exchanges of correspondence are properly recorded within your system for future reference so that you can become aware if the same customer is repeatedly raising the same or similar excuses.

Some examples of the more common form of excuses raised by delinquent customers are set out in **Document 4**, which also provides a list of appropriate replies dealing with the essential points mentioned above.

Doc. 4

Excuses and replies

Customer excuse	Suggested reply
1 We have no money. Any further pressure upon us is likely to force us into insolvency.	We are sorry to learn of your present difficulties and note that there is no dispute on the amount of our invoice or the goods/services which have been delivered/rendered. In the circumstances if you are unable to provide us with payment in full by return we will have to stop further supplies to you and to rely upon the terms of the retention of title clause in our Conditions of Sale and to require you to deliver up to us our goods which are in your possession but which as yet are not paid for. NB: The way that you treat customers in this situation may vary. Obviously if they are good customers of long standing you will be better disposed to behave sympathetically. In such cases you may prefer to talk to them informally, and to schedule a payment plan so that the debt to you is paid off over time.
2 Our company is in the middle of a huge reorganisation and the system is unable to generate cheques; *or* Our company is currently changing banks and we have no access to funds.	We appreciate the difficulties which can occur in such circumstances and note that there is no query arising on the amount of our invoices or the goods/services which have been delivered/rendered. In the circumstances, therefore, we must insist that the terms set out in our Conditions of Sale are complied with and ask you to settle these accounts in full by return. We will be quite happy to accept a manually prepared cheque or a bank draft if this is more convenient to you.
3 We do not appear to have any trace of your invoice. Please send a duplicate.	(Reply by fax) We understand that our invoice number [ ] has gone astray. We attach a copy of the original. We confirm that the goods were delivered to you on [ ] and that to date we have had no query with

Doc. 4 continued

	regard to that delivery or the condition of the goods supplied. In the circumstances we must ask for payment in full by return to ensure that we continue trading under the terms of our Conditions of Sale.
4 Our cheque signatories are all out of the office for a few days.	We are disappointed to note that all of the cheque signatories in your office appear to be unavailable for a considerable period of time. In these circumstances please let us know at once the names of the individuals within your organisation who are authorised to sign cheques, how many signatories are required and the earliest date upon which those people will be back in your office. Since the situation may occur again I think it appropriate to add to the terms upon which we continue to supply you that you arrange for the enclosed direct debit form to be signed and returned to us so that these difficulties can be avoided in future. It also seems appropriate in the meantime that further supplies from our company to yours should be stopped in accordance with our normal trading practice.
5 Our cheque is in the post.	We acknowledge your assurance that payment in full has been despatched to us but we regret to say that your cheque has not yet been received. Please let me know the date your cheque was sent, the cheque number, to which address and to whom it was posted and whether it was delivered by first class mail. We suggest that if your cheque is not received by first mail tomorrow morning we will telephone for a replacement cheque by return.
6 We are currently awaiting funds from a large customer and can only pay you when these funds are received.	While we can understand your problem we note that no query has been raised with regard to our invoices. We must therefore insist that

Doc. 4 **continued**

the terms set out in our Conditions of Sale are complied with. It would be useful, however, if you could let us have the name and address of your debtor, the amount which is owed and the expected date for payment. Have you considered making arrangements with your bank to provide additional funds on security of the debt which is owed to you? In the circumstances it seems there are means by which additional funds might be raised and we must therefore insist upon receiving your remittance by return.

IDENTIFYING PROFESSIONAL DEBTORS

Inevitably, and no matter how efficient your new system may be, there will always be a small number of customers who will use every query, complaint and excuse they can think of to postpone the evil day when they have to stump up some cash. Sooner or later you will begin to recognise them. You will already have used your query/complaint procedure on a number of occasions and your production, marketing, sales and despatch colleagues will have become more and more frustrated about having their valuable time taken up with a list of spurious enquiries.

They will have gone through all the excuses known to you (and some new ones!) and at the end of the day you will recognise that these particular customers have developed their own sophisticated system for delaying payment as long as possible.

What has to be recognised in these circumstances is that if you are pressing for payment there is quite likely to be a list of other creditors who are making similar demands and you must do something to attract this debtor's attention and get your company to the head of the queue. A letter of the type set out in **Letter 21** may do the trick. Again, it is personally addressed to the person in the organisation who is responsible for paying your accounts. You should bear in mind, however, that by the time you get to this stage you may wish to be addressing yourself to the managing director or finance director whose particulars you will already have obtained by using **Form 1**. In light of the information you are about to impart, the higher level within your customer company you can reach the better.

Letter 21 Letter to professional debtor (limited company) (for a debt over £750)

Dear

Most important – please read this letter

On [date] at 11.45am, you promised to send me a cheque postdated [date] for payment of your overdue account. You have dishonoured that promise, thereby showing that your company is unable to pay its debts as they fall due.

I may now petition for the compulsory winding up of your company under the Insolvency Act 1986 section 122(1)(f) and section 123(1)(e).

It is important you know that if this action is taken against your company, you, as a director, may be guilty of wrongful trading and so be deemed personally liable by the court (see the Insolvency Act 1986 section 214). If so, you may also be prosecuted under the Company Directors Disqualification Act 1986.

If you wish to avoid the consequences of the above please pay your account by [date].

Yours sincerely

Credit Services Manager

Amount overdue	:	£
Payment terms	:	X days from date of invoice
Account	:	123456

The principal object of **Letter 21** is to attract the attention of the professional debtor to a number of specific points as follows:

1 That you have been keeping a record of the occasions when he or she has sought to exceed credit limits.

2 That you have been recording the occasions when payment has been delayed beyond the terms of credit agreed.

3 That you have been keeping an eye on the queries and excuses for non-payment which have been raised and have noted that they have invariably been without substance.

Such behaviour by a debtor is unacceptable. What you therefore have to do is to draw your debtor's attention to areas where they may consider themselves to be vulnerable. Therefore, having checked your customer's financial records and in particular the company's accounts filed recently with the Registrar of

Companies, you may find that your customer's financial position is precarious to say the least and the company may indeed be technically insolvent and its accounts qualified accordingly. You may also find that the company's accounts have not been filed within the time limits imposed by the Companies Acts, giving you some additional ammunition to use.

If that is the case, or if the last accounts, filed a year or more ago, show a marginal position and you are aware that the customer's trading position has deteriorated substantially in the meantime, then you may be justified in suggesting that insolvency has taken place at some time in the past and that since that date, by placing orders and accepting delivery, the directors of your debtor company may have become personally liable for the liabilities which have accrued. This personal liability arises under the Insolvency Act 1986 which also provides that in the event that the debtor company is insolvent and is subsequently wound up, an adverse report may be made by the liquidator to the Department of Trade and Industry, which in turn could lead to the disqualification of those directors from holding further office in the future.

By drawing these points to their attention you are in fact carrying out an exercise in controlled queue jumping, your primary object being to get your own company ahead of other unsecured creditors who are lining up to receive what payment they can. By getting yourself to the head of the queue and receiving payment in full you are protecting your own cash position perhaps at the expense of others.

It is important to recognise, however, the seriousness of the allegations which you are raising. You should therefore ensure that the information contained in your letter is entirely accurate and to avoid the risk of publishing a defamatory statement to a third party, your letter should be addressed only to the relevant directors of your debtor company. You should also appreciate that if as a result of the pressure you are applying you receive a substantial payment from your customer just before he or she goes into bankruptcy or just before liquidation and that payment is seen by the official receiver or liquidator to prejudice the rights of recovery of other creditors, then the receiver or liquidator may attempt and be entitled to apply to you for repayment of all or part of the sums you have received on the basis that that payment amounted to an unfair preference received in priority to other unsecured creditors. While that claim may be rebuttable if payment was made for good commercial reasons – for example, to secure further supplies – it is again a point to bear in mind when considering the timing of payments received and the promptness of the steps you take for recovery.

BE FIRM BUT FAIR

At the end of the day, whether or not your system involves realistic timescales, whether it eliminates queries and complaints promptly, whether it isolates excuses and whether it identifies professional debtors and deals with them in appropriate terms, you will still be faced from time to time with customers who have in the past been loyal to your business and have paid reasonably promptly but who for one reason or another find themselves in dire financial straits and therefore are unable to comply with your current terms for payment. In those cases a larger element of commercial judgment will have to be exercised and the risks involved in extending the time for payment or for allowing further supplies will have to be set against the level of business you have done with that customer in the past and the prospect you have for doing substantial business with him or her in the future. You should take this opportunity to protect your position as best you can, perhaps by verifying that your customer is complying with the terms of your retention of title clause, and you should also ensure that all goods subsequently supplied are clearly and individually marked and kept separate from all other goods on your customer's property.

Like most other commercial decisions, however, the decision to continue to supply cannot be taken without full information as to your customer's circumstances and immediate requirements. Quite often, the only way that this can be done is by a face-to-face meeting when your customer's true financial position can be ascertained by serious consideration being given to his or her current net asset position, credit control system and debtor lists, plus the state of his or her order book and prospects of those orders being converted into profit and cash within a reasonable time frame.

If on the strength of that information you are prepared to allow your customer extended time for payment, then a letter could be written in the terms of **Letter 22**, which again is written personally to the individual with whom you are negotiating on your customer's behalf so that the personal relationship between those individuals can be confirmed. In addition, the emphasis in the letter is that an extension to your normal terms for payment has been granted and that all other terms set out in your conditions of sale will remain in force. It is also prudent at this time to attach an up-to-date statement of account showing exactly the invoices which you are talking about, confirming again specifically the terms for payment which have been agreed.

Finally, in this form of letter it is important to remind the customer that a special concession has been granted and that if he or she defaults in any way, then you reserve the right to revert to your normal payment terms and to receive repayment of all balances then outstanding, whether due for payment at that time or not. In these circumstances both parties know exactly where they are, and you will be hoping for the full benefit of the concession granted in the form of the future loyalty of a customer you have supported during hard times.

Similar kudos can be achieved by reaching agreement with your customer in the terms set out in **Letter 23**. In this letter you are agreeing to the payment of current balances by instalments, while at the same time confirming that you will only be prepared to carry on supplying products in the future either strictly in accordance with the terms of your conditions of sale, particularly with regard

Letter 22 Letter agreeing to extended terms for payment

Dear

Your request to increase payment terms

You will be pleased to know that we will agree to extend your payment terms from 30 days from date of invoice to 60 days from date of invoice.

This special concession to you is subject to future payments being made promptly. If your account falls overdue against these terms then your account will revert to our standard terms of 30 days from date of invoice and all amounts outstanding beyond this period will become immediately due for payment.

Our other Conditions of Sale remain unchanged and a copy is enclosed.

Thank you for your cooperation. I hope this new arrangement proves good for both of us.

Yours sincerely

Credit Services Manager

Amount overdue	:	£
Payment terms	:	Extended to 60 days from date of invoice
Credit limit	:	£
Account	:	123456

to payment, or on a cash against supply basis. The emphasis here is that you are allowing your customer a further concession by rescheduling his or her indebtedness to you and allowing the discharge of that indebtedness over a fixed period of time. In normal circumstances and under your conditions of sale (or, alternatively, pursuant to the statutory provisions relating to late payment) you would be entitled to charge interest on those late payments and it is of course feasible by amending the first paragraph of **Letter 23** slightly to incorporate the amount due by way of interest, either up to the time when agreement is reached or up to the time of the final instalment.

In either case, however, the basis upon which agreement is reached is that in the event that your debtor defaults in any way with regard to the payment of the agreed instalments, or in prompt payment of further invoices as they fall due, then the full amount of the balance owing by that company to yours will become immediately due for payment. Again, by recording all of these facts in correspondence any doubt remaining in the minds of the parties is wiped out and the rights reserved by your company are perfectly clear.

Letter 23 Letter agreeing to payment by instalments

Dear

Thank you for your letter of [date] together with your cheque for £300.00 in part payment of the debt of [amount]. As agreed by telephone today, your proposal to pay the account by weekly instalments is acceptable only if you send 10 postdated cheques as shown below to reach us by [date].

28.02.– –	£300.00 (received)
06.03.– –	£300.00
13.03.– –	£300.00
20.03.– –	£300.00
27.03.– –	£300.00
03.04.– –	£300.00
10.04.– –	£300.00
17.04.– –	£300.00
24.04.– –	£300.00
01.05.– –	£300.00
08.05.– –	£319.89
Total	£3,319.89

If any cheque is dishonoured on first presentation for payment then the whole debt will immediately fall due for payment.

No more supplies will be made to you until the debt is paid in full. I am glad we have been able to settle this amicably.

Yours sincerely

Credit Services Manager

Amount overdue	:	£3,319.89
Payment terms	:	X days from date of invoice
Credit limit	:	£
Account	:	123456

Collection methods

STAFF TRAINING

Once the structure of your new collection system has been set up it is vital to ensure that all of your staff connected with that system are aware of the timescales involved and what their contribution is likely to be in the collection process. Your collection timetable may be something like this:

Telephone:	With new (regular) customers get into the good habit of telephoning every two weeks for the first three months.
Invoice:	Use first class post, or courier very large invoices. On very large invoices, telephone or fax to agree that your invoice has been received.
Overdue debts:	List your accounts in value order, with the largest first. Record action on this list, together with any payments received.
Telephone:	Telephone all large accounts, the largest first. Follow up within the same month if the debt remains unpaid. If your normal contact fails, speak to someone more senior.
Send letters:	Send letters to all those you do not have the time to telephone: *Demand letter 1*: polite first reminder; *Demand letter 2*: strong final demand.
Send faxes:	Send faxes when your letters and telephone calls are being ignored. Send them to a senior person.
Send a statutory demand:	Do this only for large undisputed debts. Use only as a last resort when standard efforts have failed.
Threaten third-party action:	Do so in your second (and last) reminder letter. You could refer to a collection agency, a solicitor or court action.
Remember:	If you use a statutory demand or legal action, you lose your customer. Before resorting to either, ask your MD to speak to your customer's counterpart.

Clearly, the efforts of your sales, accounts and despatch departments will have to be coordinated to ensure that the invoice goes out at the right time. Your accounts department, if it is responsible for the issue of the statement, will have to liaise with the credit department to ensure that the statement and reminder cycle begins at the right time and obviously the sales, accounts and credit departments will have to liaise to ensure that any payments received are properly and promptly recorded in the right place at the right time so that embarrassing reminders for payments already received are not sent out.

To the same end, it is advisable that the members of the sales, accounting and credit departments are aware of the internal systems of the others, so that unfortunate lapses, such as one department dealing with complaints without reference elsewhere which could give customers another excuse to avoid prompt payment, can be avoided. Your staff should also be made aware of the problems which arise from time to time affecting their colleagues' performance and the pressures which the production and sales departments, in particular, are under to achieve their own targets. Provided that this level of understanding is maintained, the chasing process can continue in line with your company's policy.

If you are charging interest on the outstanding debt, you should notify your customer that if payment is not received then the rate of interest prescribed by your conditions of sale, or alternatively that prescribed by the statutory provisions relating to late payment of commercial debts, will be charged on that balance from the date of invoice. By specifying the current rate to be charged the attention of your customer is being drawn specifically to the further expenses which are being incurred for his or her company by this delay (see **Letter 24**).

Letter 24 Sample reminder letter claiming interest

Dear

Your Account No.

Balance Due: £

I note that I have not heard from you in reply to our recent statements and my previous letter dated [ ]. I also note that no queries have been raised on your account so the balance remaining must be undisputed.

In these circumstances I must ask you to send me by return of post your remittance for the remaining outstanding shown above. If I do not hear from you as requested then I will have no alternative but to apply interest to that balance at the rate of [ ]% per annum as prescribed by our Conditions of Sale.

Yours sincerely

Credit Manager

If no reply is received, then in accordance with your established timescales your final reminder letter is despatched setting out not only the balance then due but also any interest which has accrued from the invoice date as a result of your customer's continued default (see **Letter 26** below). The additional sanction now being applied of course is that you are now obliged to inform your sales department that no further services or goods should be supplied to that

Letter 25 Sample reminder letter stopping supplies

Dear

Notice of stop on supplies

Payment of your account from [date] has not been received. No purchase orders from your company will be acted upon while payment is still outstanding.

Under our Conditions of Sale, interest at the rate of [%] is now being charged to your account from the date when the invoices fell due for payment.

If full payment is not received by [date] then the next step is court action against you. Our Conditions of Sale also allow us to charge you with any costs incurred enforcing payment of your debt.

Please pay now.

Yours sincerely

Credit Services Manager

Amount overdue	:	£
Payment terms	:	X days from date of invoice
Credit limit	:	£
Account	:	123456

customer until the account, with all interest due, has been paid in full. **Letter 25** gives notice of this situation to your debtor.

Some companies use debt collection agencies or specialist solicitors at appropriate stages of the collection process. Whether you do so or not will depend on your company policy.

The ultimate sanction to be imposed by your credit management team in the event of persistent delay in payment is to give notice of your intention to take legal proceedings. Some companies prefer this letter to be written by their solicitors, but strictly speaking there is no need to do so. This hesitation is caused by the fact that if no prior warning is given before court proceedings are issued and served upon the debtor, and payment is made either between the date of issue and the date of service of those proceedings or immediately after the service of those proceedings, the debtor may argue that since no warning had been given that those proceedings were to be issued he or she should not be liable for the costs which you have incurred in taking that action.

Moreover, since the introduction of the 'Woolf Reforms', it has now become clear that there will be a 'pre-action protocol' for commercial debt claims. A 'letter of claim' will be an essential element of the protocol process. At the time of writing, no protocol had been finalised and no standard form of such a letter had been agreed, though drafting was in progress. **Letter 26** incorporates the elements that such a 'letter of claim' was expected to require. This letter, and your other records (reminders, notes of telephone conversations, etc.), will provide a firm foundation for your case if legal action proves to be necessary. (Bear in mind, however, that if your customer truly *cannot* pay, because they have no money, taking court action will not change the situation!)

Letter 26 sets out clearly the balance due, how it is made up, the details of all the invoices involved, a reasonable period – say seven days – within which the debtor must respond, the required method of payment, contact address and telephone number, and notice that court action will ensue if there is no response (including a claim for solicitor's costs, court fees and interest).

Letter 26

Letter before action

Dear

Court action will be the consequence of your ignoring this letter.

Despite our telephone conversations on [dates] and our letters of [dates], and your promise to pay, payment of your account has still not been received. If full payment is not received by [date] court action will be taken against you. If you allow this to happen you will incur court costs, [the court rate of interest of 8%] [statutory interest of 8% above base rate pursuant to the Late Payment of Commercial Debts (Interest) Act 1998*] from [the date the invoices fell due for payment], and you may forfeit your credit status because your name will be recorded by the major credit reference agencies. This may deter others from supplying you.

To stop this from happening please pay in full now or contact me to put forward your proposals.

Yours sincerely

Credit Services Manager

Amount overdue	:	£
Payment terms	:	X days from date of invoice
Credit limit	:	£
Account	:	123456

**Check that this Act applies to you.*

Provided with proper training in credit management and a clear credit policy supported by the directors in your company, your credit control staff will then be fully equipped to deal with most, if not all, of the issues which are likely to arise in the course of their jobs and the ruses which are likely to be exploited by your debtors on more or less a daily basis. Of course, there is nothing like experience to establish 'a feel' for problems which are likely to arise on a particular account, with a particular customer or in a particular market sector. Until that experience develops, however, the framework and objectives you have provided together with the ammunition which is available in the form of the information and letters we have considered thus far will stand your staff in good stead.

CHASING BY TELEPHONE

Having provided a basic collection structure and timescale by setting up a system of memoranda, forms and letters to be used either internally to respond to queries raised or externally as reminders to customers, many companies augment their system by telephoning customers for payment as part of the collection process. This method is one of the more effective cash collection procedures in that it has a basic advantage over letter-writing by making direct and personal contact with an individual in the customer's organisation and requiring from him or her an answer to a specific query. The query is:

When are we going to be paid?

and the answer sought should be equally direct.

Because of time constraints it may not be feasible to contact all your customers by telephone to chase up payment of every overdue invoice or series of payments due. Many companies therefore decide to use telephone collection for accounts overdue above a particular value or for debts older than a certain age. Whatever the system, there are certain basic requirements which are essential to make telephone collection effective. They are as follows:

1 *Be prepared.* You already have on your system all the information you require to make your call. You have the name and telephone number of your contact, you have details of any invoices overdue for payment and you should be aware of any existing queries which are causing delay. You should therefore be in a position to answer at once any particular points which are raised by your customer.
2 *Be courteous.* Remember that every contact your company makes with your customer can add to your existing relationship, and even a collection call, if carried out pleasantly and properly, can add to that process. Even when dealing with queries, complaints or excuses it is possible by adopting a standard, well-rehearsed routine to appear friendly and professional at all times, thereby earning your customer's respect and ultimately his or her loyalty.

3 *Be precise.* Ensure that you are dealing only with invoices which are currently due for payment and that you are not encouraging the customer to raise red herrings by pursuing a claim for payment which is already under query, or which has already been dealt with either by a part-payment or credit note. Your precision should extend to the maintenance of accurate records of your telephone calls and in Form 9 is set out a useful telephone collection sheet which can be used to monitor the progress of your discussion with a particular customer using this system. (**Forms 6 (a)** and **(b)** may also provide alternative layouts for this purpose.) The basic information is of course obtained from the customer's initial application for a credit facility (**Form 1**), as well as the additional information gleaned from your customer history record sheet (**Form 6**).

4 *Be firm but sympathetic.* Remember that your opposite numbers in your customer's bought ledger department will also have limitations on the control they have over their own affairs, dependent largely on the influence of their own business leaders. If they are instructed to delay payment or are told to make payments in a certain order then there may be little you can do to persuade them towards a different course of action. On the other hand, if you are sympathetic then on occasion you may be able to persuade them to give your outstanding invoices priority over other creditors if they have some leeway, or in the absence of a specific directive from above.

Form 9

Telephone collection sheet

(Forms 6(a) and (b) may also help to provide alternative layouts for this purpose)

Customer name: Credit manager:
Credit limit: £   Opening date:
Account No.

Invoice dates	Total balance £	Balance currently due: £
Contact name	Telephone number	Status
Time of call 1. 2. 3. 4. 5.	Date of call 1. 2. 3. 4. 5.	Date of last payment and amount

Responses received:
Call No. 1.
2.
3.
4.
5.

REACHING AGREEMENT

In the course of discussions between your credit managers and your customers a considerable amount of negotiation will take place either in relation to queries and complaints which are raised by your customer or in the event that your customer has some other difficulty in paying, caused perhaps by his or her own cash flow problems. This means that your customer may be persuading you to accept part-payments or payments by instalments while at the same time ordering further supplies from you. Again, in the course of these discussions it is vital to ensure that the position of your company is accurately recorded at all times. So, for example, if you are merely in the process of exchanging opening negotiations with your customer about one or two queries on his or her account, while at the same time the customer is trying to persuade you to accept a part-payment because of his or her cash flow problems, or indeed part-payment as full settlement of the balance due to you, you may wish to use a letter such as **Letter 27** to confirm the position from your side of the fence.

In that letter your credit manager is again addressing the individual with whom he or she is dealing and confirming the balance due on the account. The letter acknowledges receipt of a cheque towards the balance which is due but confirms that the total amount required is greater than the payment received so that the remaining balance is clearly set out. The letter goes on to confirm that

Letter 27

Letter acknowledging part-payment

Dear

Thank you for your cheque for [amount] which has been accepted in part payment of your account. This still leaves an amount of £[ ] overdue.

If you have cash flow problems please contact us to agree a payment plan for the balance of your account. If not, and to enable us to continue to supply you, we must ask you to honour the conditions of our current agreement and send your payment to reach us by [date].

Yours sincerely

Credit Services Manager

Amount overdue	:	£
Payment terms	:	X days from date of invoice
Credit limit	:	£
Account	:	123456

no specific query has been raised in relation to the supplies rendered and repeats the insistence upon a cheque for the balance outstanding by return. This leaves the debtor in the position where he or she is fully aware of your stance, and while during the course of your discussions you may be persuaded to allow a discount or some other form of credit against the balance which remains, as far as your strict contractual position is concerned you have made this clear.

In the course of your negotiations and following the enquiries which you have undertaken about a query or complaint raised by your customer, you may wish, in order to accelerate the payment of at least part of the sum due to you, to put forward a proposal for final settlement. It may be that if your proposal is not accepted by your debtor, you would not wish to have the offer raised in evidence in any subsequent court proceedings since it may imply that you are admitting liability to all or part of your customer's claims.

Such an offer, however, can be made on a 'without prejudice' basis and **Letter 28** shows how this can be done. The letter is again addressed specifically to the person with whom you are negotiating and it is headed boldly at the top

Letter 28

Letter confirming 'without prejudice' discussions

Dear

Without Prejudice

Balance in dispute £[ ].

Thank you for bringing to my attention your dissatisfaction with the quality of some of our goods/services. We are sorry that we have not met your expectations on this occasion. To compensate you, this is our 'without prejudice' proposal:

That:

- the amount in dispute above is reduced by 5%; and
- if this is acceptable to you, the remaining balance is paid by [date]; and
- you confirm in writing that your payment is in full and final settlement of all outstanding disputes between us concerning the above amount.

I do hope that you find this acceptable and that we can then put this matter behind us. Thank you for giving us the opportunity to settle this amicably.

Yours sincerely

Credit Services Manager

Amount overdue	:	£
Payment terms	:	X days from date of invoice
Credit limit	:	£
Account	:	123456

'without prejudice'. This phrase is designed to draw to the attention of the person to whom the offer is made that the proposal is put forward in an effort to settle outstanding matters between you and is not intended to form any admission as to liability, or to allow any statement which the letter may contain to be allowed to prejudice the rights or wrongs of your case at the end of the day.

In that letter, therefore, you can again confirm the position between your respective companies and without adversely affecting your case record the outcome of your own enquiries. It is then open to you to make some form of offer to settle the difficulties which have arisen, for example by reducing the amount of your claim by a certain percentage, but again to ensure that your momentum is maintained it is important that you leave that offer of settlement open only for a short period of time within which payment of the discounted balance should be made in full. Provided payment is made within the time limit allowed, you indicate that you will accept the reduced sum in full and final settlement of all outstanding issues remaining between your respective companies, which would include of course any claim your customer may have against you for any damages or other losses arising as a result of the delivery of defective goods or the provision of negligent services.

It is perfectly proper for your customer to accept the proposal set out in your 'without prejudice' letter and if he or she does so then that agreement will be binding upon you both. You should not make the mistake of thinking (as do many companies and some lawyers!) that provided an offer is set out in 'without prejudice' correspondence, any acceptance of that offer is not binding upon the party making it.

If your offer is accepted then you have a contract but it is still useful to send a letter such as that set out in **Letter 29** confirming the agreement which has

Letter 29 Letter confirming settlement

Dear

Many thanks for your cheque [amount] and your letter of [date] confirming that it is payment in full and final settlement of the debt totalling [amount] previously disputed.

Now that this is behind us we would like the chance to prove we can provide products/services that fully match your expectations. I have already spoken to our sales people about this and they will be contacting you soon.

Thank you again for your help in settling this matter amicably.

Yours sincerely

Credit Services Manager

been reached. That letter is designed to confirm that the payment made by your customer, and which no doubt has been offered in full and final settlement of all outstanding balances and issues remaining between your companies, is accepted upon those terms and the letter is designed to act as a formal receipt for that payment. The second paragraph of that letter is intended to assist both parties to 'bury the hatchet' and to continue the business relationship which previously existed.

It may be that the terms of settlement reached between you and your customer will incorporate extended terms for future payment, or an agreement to accept payment for current liabilities by instalments. In those instances the appropriate parts of **Letters** 22 and 23 should be incorporated into your letters confirming settlement so that the full terms agreed are accurately recorded.

Enforcing your rights

There is little point in setting up a series of contractual responsibilities and obligations between you and your customer and creating a framework to speed up the process of collecting money due to your company unless both you and your staff are fully aware of all the rights and liabilities which are likely to arise under the system you have created. You must also be prepared to enforce those rights to protect your company's position. You will recall that apart from taking out some form of credit insurance policy the principal methods of securing payment of domestic (that is UK) invoices is either to include within your conditions of sale a fully enforceable retention of title clause, or alternatively to seek from the customer some form of guarantee either from a holding company or subsidiary or from one of its directors.

RETENTION OF TITLE CLAUSES

How then does one enforce a claim that title in certain goods has not passed because payment in full has not been made? Under the terms of a retention of title clause, until the property (that is to say, title or ownership) in the goods has passed to the buyer, the seller should be entitled at any time to require the buyer to redeliver the goods to the seller, and if he or she fails to do so the seller is then entitled to enter upon any premises where the goods are stored and take possession of them. It is crucial to the successful enforcement of retention of title rights that the seller is able conclusively to identify his/her goods held by the buyer. The use of serial numbers and other distinguishing marks or labels on the goods is a highly recommended practice for the seller.

The emphasis of course is on the fact that ownership has not passed to the buyer, but this may take place in spite of the terms of the retention of title clause if, as has been indicated earlier, the buyer has merged the goods with others of his or her own or if work has been carried out which has added to their value. On the assumption that the buyer has not, however, then a starting point is for your credit manager to give notice under your retention of title clause requiring the immediate delivery of certain specific goods which have not been paid for. By using a letter of the type set out in **Letter 30**, which again is addressed directly to his or her opposite number, your credit manager specifies the grounds upon which title to the goods is claimed and demands their redelivery. Your customer is required to take immediate steps to redeliver the specific goods listed in your delivery notes, or alternatively a list of goods which can be scheduled to the letter. Your credit manager also requires a list of any goods which your customer may have sold on and demands an immediate payment for the proceeds of those sales. The letter makes it clear that any rights which the customer may have enjoyed to use the goods or resell them are revoked. As a consequence of the revocation of these rights, if the customer proceeds to resell, consume or otherwise deal with the goods, you may be able to take legal action for damages for wrongful interference and/or conversion of

Letter 30 Letter exercising your retention of title clause

Dear

Your Account No.
Balance Due: £

I am disappointed to note that, in spite of our recent discussions and the statements and letters I have sent to you, the outstanding balance on your account remains substantially overdue for payment.

In the circumstances and in accordance with Clause [ ] of our Conditions of Sale, title in the goods delivered remains with us and, under the terms of that Clause, we are entitled to demand from you the return of those goods or, if they have been sold on, the money which you have received from that sale.

Please make arrangements for the immediate redelivery to us of the goods listed in Delivery Notes numbered [–] (copies enclosed) together with a Schedule identifying any goods which you have sold on and your remittance for the proceeds of such sales. Any rights which you may previously have had to resell or consume the goods are hereby revoked. You must continue, pending the redelivery of our goods, to hold our goods separately stored as our fiduciary agent and bailee.

Regrettably, if this is not done by [date], I will have no alternative but [to make appropriate arrangements for the collection of those goods from your site] [to refer the matter to our solicitors to take such action as may be available to us to protect our position which may include legal action for wrongful interference with, or conversion of, our goods in breach of the Torts (Interference with Goods) Act 1977].

Yours sincerely

Credit Manager

the goods under the provisions of the Torts (Interference with Goods) Act 1977. Finally, the letter gives notice that if your customer has not replied by return, then your credit manager will make alternative arrangements for the collection of the goods or reserve other courses of action which may be open.

It has to be said that the disadvantage of writing such a letter is that it puts your customer immediately on notice of the rights you are claiming. In some instances it may be prudent for your retention of title clause specifically to entitle you to retake possession of the goods without providing this form of notice. Again, much depends on the relationship you have with a particular customer at a particular time and the prospects you may have for a trading relationship at some time in the future. If you choose to proceed without notice, then the sight of your lorries appearing at your customer's factory gates and taking away the raw materials or components which are essential to his or her business may have a traumatic and long-lasting effect! On the other hand, if you feel that any kind of warning is likely to result in your customer taking evasive action by removing the goods or by selling them on quickly, albeit at a much reduced price, then early action may be commended.

CALLING IN GUARANTEES

If in the course of carrying out your credit assessment of your customer you have been wise enough to obtain guarantees from holding or subsidiary companies, or from one or more of the directors of your customer company, then in the event that your customer defaults the letters set out in **Letters 31** and **32** should be used to call upon those guarantees for the balance outstanding. These letters should be addressed to one or more directors of the subsidiary or holding company concerned, or to the guaranteeing director personally – preferably

Letter 31 Letter calling on a guarantee (company)

Dear Sir or Madam

Your Subsidiary: Limited
Account No.
Balance Outstanding: £

You will recall that by letter of guarantee dated [ ] your Company undertook to us that in the event of a default by your above named subsidiary you would indemnify us in respect of any loss, damages and costs arising as a result.

Although under the terms of the indemnity given by you to us, we have no obligation to pursue the above company for payment of the balance outstanding, we regret to advise you that, despite repeated reminders, the above company has failed to pay the outstanding balance shown above which has now been overdue for some considerable time.

In these circumstances we must now call upon you to satisfy the terms of your guarantee by paying to us the above amount by [date]. If full payment is not received by [date], we will instruct our Solicitors to take proceedings against you for the full amount of our claim plus interest and costs and we confirm that such proceedings will be taken without further notice to you.

If you have any queries, please contact me.

Yours faithfully

Credit Manager

Letter 32 Letter calling on a guarantee (directors)

Dear Sir or Madam

Company: Limited
Account No.
Balance Outstanding: £

You will recall that by letter of guarantee dated [ ] you undertook to us that in the event of a default by the above named company you would indemnify us in respect of any loss, damages and costs arising as a result.

Although under the terms of the indemnity given by you to us, we have no obligation to pursue the above company for payment of the balance outstanding, we regret to advise you that, despite repeated reminders, the above company has failed to pay the outstanding balance shown above which has now been overdue for some considerable time.

In these circumstances we must now call upon you to satisfy the terms of your guarantee by paying to us the above amount by [date]. If full payment is not received by [date], we will instruct our Solicitors to take proceedings against you for the full amount of our claim plus interest and costs and we confirm that such proceedings will be taken without further notice to you.

If you have any queries, please contact me.

Yours faithfully

Credit Manager

at the home address you have obtained on the original application for a credit facility in **Form 1**. The letters specify which company is indebted to you, give the account number and the balance outstanding and remind the director to whom you are writing of the terms of the guarantee which has been given. Although there is no obligation under the guarantees set out in **Letters 8** and **9** to press the guaranteed company for payment (that is because the guarantee itself is expressed to be a primary obligation by the guarantor similar to that of indemnity), it is useful to confirm that repeated reminders have been delivered and no response has been obtained.

The final main paragraph in each case is a formal demand for the terms of the guarantee to be satisfied within a specific time, advising that if no response is received within that time then solicitors will be instructed to take proceedings without further notice.

Going legal

In the event that all your collection procedures and techniques have been frustrated and the time limits set by your initial collection objectives have expired, the decision may ultimately be forced upon you that the only method of collection of a particular debt is to resort to legal action.

INSTRUCTING SOLICITORS

It is important, of course, to remember that the principal objective of suing is still to obtain payment of the outstanding balance due to your company and in instructing your solicitor or legal department to take legal proceedings the information you have obtained must be properly and accurately transmitted. **Form 10** is designed to provide a straightforward format in which all the relevant information required by your solicitor can be presented as clearly and succinctly as possible but at the same time ensuring the degree of accuracy which is required under the new Civil Procedure Rules introduced as part of the 'Woolf Reforms' from 26 April 1999.

Form 10 Form of instruction to solicitors

Debt Collection Department

NAME OF CREDITOR ....
TRADING ADDRESS ....
REGISTERED OFFICE (if different) ....
CONTACT NAME ....
NAME OF DEBTOR ....
Is the Debtor an individual, firm or company? ....
REGISTERED NUMBER (if a company)...
REGISTERED OFFICE ....
TRADING ADDRESS (if different) ....
AMOUNT OF DEBT ....(inclusive of VAT)
Does debt relate to goods sold and delivered, services rendered or other?
If other please specify
DATE & NUMBERS OF INVOICES ....
....
DATES & AMOUNTS OF PAYMENTS ....
....
How many days after delivery of Invoice was payment due? ....
Are Invoices disputed? ....
If yes, please provide copies of relevant correspondence
(If possible Debtor's letterheading will assist)
Have any cheques paid to you been dishonoured? ....
Are you aware of the location of any specific assets? ....
Do you have any special instructions?...

There may be a range of legal action available to your company but in each case, whether your proceedings are to be issued in the High Court, in the County Court, or whether your claim is to be pursued by statutory demand and then by bankruptcy or winding-up proceedings, because such actions are considered to be extremely serious from your debtor's point of view, any inaccuracies which creep into your action will only be to your debtor's advantage. It is therefore vital to make quite certain that the information you are passing over is accurate and up to date.

For example, it is important to ensure that the name under which you are suing matches up exactly with the name of the company or trading division within your organisation with whom your customer originally contracted. You should therefore check the original contract and invoice documentation to ensure that the name of the creditor (and therefore the claimant) which you give to your solicitor is confirmed by your documentation. If there have been any internal changes or reorganisations within your business, this information should also be passed on to ensure that the proceedings are issued on behalf of the correct legal entity even though its name may have changed in the meantime.

For similar reasons it is vital to make sure that the name and status of your debtor is properly identified. Innumerable cases brought before the High Court and County Court are dismissed at an early stage with costs being awarded against the claimant when the defendant is able to show that proceedings have been taken against the wrong party, or that the status of the party being sued is incorrect. It is therefore essential to be aware of whether your customer is trading as a sole proprietor, as a firm, or as a company, and if you are dealing with individuals whether that individual is male or female. Any inaccuracy here can undermine your claim completely.

It is also important to ensure that your solicitor is given the addresses of any location where your customer is or has been trading. In the case of sole proprietors or partners it is useful to have their home addresses in case the businesses cease trading. This will assist with any future enforcement of your judgment. The immediate target in any legal action you bring is to obtain judgment in your favour for the full amount of your claim plus interest and costs. Such judgments can be obtained if your customer fails to file an acknowledgment of service or a defence to the claim within the relevant time for doing so: this is referred to as a 'default judgment'. Once that judgment is obtained, however, your solicitor will need certain information to be accurately and readily available from you if that judgment is to be properly enforced.

It may seem obvious, but clear instructions must also be given as to the amount of debt which is due, and whether the debt has arisen as a result of goods sold and delivered, services rendered or work done and materials supplied. It is always useful for your solicitors to be given copies of your invoices as well as details of the dates, numbers and payments due under each.

By receiving the information in **Form 10**, that is to say the dates when payments fell due and whether any of the invoices are disputed, your solicitor will be able to frame your court proceedings in a manner which will narrow any outstanding issues remaining between you and your customer, while at the same time claiming the full amount for which your customer is liable, including interest at the predetermined contractual or statutory rate. If your customer has presented cheques to you for payment and those cheques have subsequently been dishonoured, then that may give rise to a separate cause of action to which your customer may have no defence whatsoever.

As in most cases therefore the information you have been able to obtain in the course of your dealings with your customer is vital, and one of the main pieces of information which will be of relevance to you and to your solicitor in the legal process will be your customer's ability to pay.

At the outset of your dealings with that customer you will have carried out a full credit check and it is worth going through that process again before your proceedings are issued. The reason for this is simply that while it is a relatively simple process to obtain judgment in the absence of a strong defence, it is often much more difficult to enforce that judgment and obtain payment, particularly if the judgment debtor has few assets which are capable of being realised quickly into hard cash. The following checklist is therefore useful:

1 What is the exact nature of the debt and is it likely to be disputed?
2 Are you certain as to the identity of the debtor and his or her legal status?
3 Is your debtor worth suing at all?

THE DECISION TO WRITE OFF

Having gone through your various collection procedures in accordance with your required timescales, and having taken all steps up to and perhaps including the institution of legal proceedings in an effort to collect the funds which are properly due to you, you may at some stage be forced towards a decision to write off all or part of your customer's liability for any one of the following reasons:

1 The amount which you claim may be disputed and the costs involved pursuing that claim through the courts may be prohibitive or even exceed the amount of your claim.
2 You may be aware through your own enquiries that your debtor has no available funds or realisable assets to satisfy the amount of the debt.
3 Your customer may have ceased trading, changed location or disappeared altogether.
4 The identity of your debtor and his or her legal status may be in some doubt. If you have not checked his or her true identity or creditworthiness you may find, for example, that you are dealing with a company with no assets as opposed to an individual of some substance.

5 You may find that the action you have taken is too late if a receiver has been appointed, for example by your debtor's bank, or if a liquidator has been appointed as a result of winding-up proceedings.

In each of these cases there may be little point in your incurring further expense in continuing your collection process and in particular incurring further costs and expenses which will arise in the course of legal proceedings. It is probably far better for you to take the hard decision to stop action and to write off the debt sooner rather than later so that the resources of your credit management team can be directed towards the recovery of claims that are likely to be satisfied.

In the course of the writing-off process you should of course bear in mind the implications of that action on other parts of your business. For example, it may lead to demand for repayment under a factoring agreement (see Chapter 12), or it may put your company in breach of its obligations under a credit insurance policy. There are also tax implications in the writing-off process and you should ensure for example that any VAT recoverable is claimed at the end of six months after the original date of supply of the goods. Your bad debt provisions will also need to be adjusted accordingly.

ENFORCING JUDGMENT – ALTERNATIVE METHODS

If court action has been taken and a judgment for the full amount of your claim has been entered against your debtor, whether that has been achieved because he or she has not properly defended your claim or because a judge has decided in your favour on the weight of evidence available, the next and equally important step will be the conversion of that judgment into cash.

The most common method is an application for a warrant of execution by which the court bailiff (in County Court proceedings) or the sheriff's officer (usually in High Court proceedings) will seize and sell goods belonging to a judgment debtor. While on occasion the threat of a forced sale will sometimes produce payment, it is important again to ensure that the right information is given so that costs are not wasted. Quite often, the sheriff's officer is directed in the first instance to the registered office rather than the principal trading address of the company. This may either be the address of a solicitor or accountant, or if it is the address of the company's headquarters it may only contain office equipment, which in any event may be leased or on hire purchase, or otherwise be of very limited value.

In those instances it may be appropriate for you or your solicitor to write to the sheriff's officer in the terms described in **Letter 33**.

This letter sets out the names of the parties, the case number, the judgment number and the execution number used by the sheriff. It also sets out clearly the amount outstanding, which should include interest and costs to date. It will be extremely useful from the sheriff's point of view if you are able to specify

Letter 33 Letter to sheriff's officer

Dear Sheriff

Case Number :
Claim Number :
Amount Outstanding :

Further to correspondence with your office, I would like to offer you some further information to assist in the successful execution of my warrant.

My enquiries show that the judgment debtor is still trading. The following may be helpful. [*delete items marked with an asterisk as appropriate*]

Credit Application*
I enclose a copy of the judgment debtor's credit application giving further information which may be relevant including [credit card details/mobile phone number/bank account details*].

In the past I have accepted/refused* cheques from the judgment debtor which have been met on presentation.

Company Accounts*
I enclose an extract of accounts for the judgment debtor company showing the registered office and trading address – please attend at the trading address to secure a levy.

Assets*
Assets can be found at [new address] which is within your county – please attend at this new address immediately and levy any goods which are found to belong to the debtor. If you cannot achieve a levy please photograph the premises/goods and send me your full report at the agreed fixed fee of £50.00 plus VAT.

Hours of Trading*
The defendant trades on a Saturday/evenings/early morning at [new address] – please ask the Sheriff's Officer to attend out of normal working hours to secure a levy. If a levy cannot be achieved please photograph the premises and send me your full report.

Vehicles*
I believe the defendant has a motor vehicle registered in his name. Please would you attempt to levy execution on this vehicle and carry out a DVLA search to confirm that the defendant is the 'registered keeper'. If you discover that this vehicle is on lease/hire purchase please send me full details.

We would be grateful if you would arrange for the judgment to be enforced as a matter of urgency. Please liaise with me/[my solicitor] direct on any further information you obtain following your attendance which may assist in securing payment of our judgment debt.

Yours sincerely

Credit Manager

which of the debtor's assets are at which addresses and if you can confirm that the debtor is continuing to trade from those addresses so that the sheriff can enter there during normal business hours.

Again, most of this information should be available to you from your current records or at least from enquiries which can be made by your representatives who are used to dealing with your former customer direct.

In the event that the execution process is unsuccessful, or indeed if you feel that it is not worthwhile bothering with at all, it may be that your enquiries have identified another company or business who owes money in turn to your judgment debtor. That indebtedness can be claimed by your company by taking what are known as garnishee proceedings through the courts. This is a procedure by which an order can be sought from the court that the money owed to your judgment debtor can be paid to you direct.

Bear in mind, however, that in essence a new set of legal proceedings will be required to obtain a garnishee order, and that further costs and delay are likely. Following judgment an application can be made to the court for an attachment of earnings order. The defendant is initially given the opportunity to have a suspended attachment of earnings order. This means that the full order is not given direct to the employer as long as the defendant maintains the monthly payments to the court. If, however, the defendant fails to make any of the agreed payments under the suspended order, the full order can be obtained and will be sent to the employer. Thereafter, monies will be deducted at source.

Such an order will direct your debtor's employer to deduct a specific weekly or monthly amount from the debtor's salary and pay it to you, via the court office. Obviously, the court will need to assess a figure which it feels the debtor will need by way of income on a regular basis to meet his or her usual commitments.

As in all these cases, the implication is firmly that the instalments you receive are likely to be fairly minimal, particularly in the case of debtors who have a low level of remuneration. In the case of such a debtor who regularly changes employment, the experience can lead more to frustration and high blood pressure than to any effective method of debt recovery.

One further enforcement procedure is available to your company in the event that your debtor owns or has an interest in property. This procedure, known as an application for a charging order, has the effect of securing the judgment debt obtained against that property. Of necessity it is only of any value if the charge can be converted into cash by a subsequent application to the court for an order for sale of the property, and if the property providing the security has sufficient equity (for example, after the payment of a prior mortgage) to cover the amount of your claim.

Again, any application to be made on these grounds must be founded upon the basis of confirmed information retained through your systems and made available to your solicitors at the right time.

BANKRUPTCY AND WINDING-UP

If all other methods of enforcement have failed, or in your view are likely to fail, then the only alternative available to you as judgment creditor may be to begin insolvency proceedings to wind up your debtor company or to make your debtor bankrupt if he or she is an individual or a partner of a firm and if the debt is greater than £750. If your insolvency action is begun after an unsatisfied bailiff/sheriff execution, then no further demand for payment is required and your petition will be presented to the court and an application for liquidation of the company or for a bankruptcy order will be dealt with accordingly. If you have not taken enforcement steps with the bailiff/sheriff then a statutory demand will need to be served to the individual debtor before a petition can be issued. In the case of a limited company a further letter of demand will need to be served under the provisions of the Insolvency Act 1986, s.123 (1)(e). This will lead to the appointment of a liquidator of the company's affairs or an official receiver of an individual's affairs, who will be responsible for the realisation of its assets and the distribution of funds received among the remaining creditors once the cost of the liquidation proceedings, together with any amounts owed to preferential or secured creditors, have been paid in full. Almost inevitably, a trading creditor will be totally unsecured and may therefore be faced with the prospect of a payment out of a few pence for each pound he or she is owed. The same is likely to apply in bankruptcy proceedings when the official receiver is responsible for the realisation of the bankrupt's assets and the payment out to his or her creditors. Many creditors therefore do not consider the instigation of bankruptcy or winding-up proceedings to be a very lucrative course of action.

More increasingly in recent years, however, and particularly since the Insolvency Act 1986, the threat of winding-up proceedings or personal bankruptcy in particular has been used as an effective addition to the weapons in the credit manager's armoury. A form of statutory demand as required by the Insolvency Act 1986 requiring payment within 21 days may be threatened or served by your credit management team as an alternative to the issue of court proceedings, in an effort to accelerate the payment of outstanding accounts which are properly due. This practice is, however, rightly frowned upon and is an abuse of process unless issued following a judgment against the debtor. It may therefore put you at risk as to costs. It may be that a letter in the terms set out in **Letter 34** may be a useful preliminary to the real thing, especially if you are dealing with a long-established customer who you know is having particular problems and whom you would not like to see going to the wall. **Letter 34** sets out in basic terms the efforts which have been made to enforce the judgment debt, it gives full particulars of the balance outstanding including the principal sum, interest and costs incurred, and indicates that unless some effort towards payment is made by the judgment debtor then insolvency proceedings would be inevitable.

Letter 34

Letter to debtor giving notice of intention to issue winding-up proceedings

Dear

Judgment No.
Debt outstanding £

Despite attempts to enforce the judgment obtained against you, the above debt, which includes interest and court costs, remains unpaid.

Our next action is to start winding-up proceedings against you under the Insolvency Act 1986 sections 122(1)(f) and 123(1)(e).

You can stop this from happening by contacting us by [date] with an acceptable proposal to pay your account.

Yours sincerely

Credit Services Manager

If ignored, this would lead immediately to the service of a statutory demand upon your debtor as set out in **Form 11(a)** for companies and **11(b)** for individuals, which are the statutory forms prescribed by the Insolvency Act 1986. The form demands payment of the debt in full within a period of 21 days, failing which the judgment creditor will be at liberty to issue a petition to the court for an order that the debtor company be wound up and a liquidator appointed.

Form 11(a) Statutory demand (company)

Reproduced by kind permission of the Solicitor's Law Stationery Society

Statutory Demand under section 123(1)(a) or 222(1)(a) of the Insolvency Act 1986 No. 4.1* (Rule 4.5)

WARNING

- This is an **important** document. This demand must be dealt with **within 21 days** after its service upon the company or a winding-up order could be made in respect of the company.
- Please read the demand and notes carefully.

DEMAND

To

Address

This demand is served on you by the Creditor:

Name

Address

The Creditor claims that the Company owes the sum of £ ,full particulars of which are set out on page 2.

The Creditor demands that the Company do pay the above debt or secure or compound for it to the Creditor's satisfaction.

Signature of individual

Name
(BLOCK LETTERS)

Dated

*Position with or relationship to Creditor

*I am authorised to make this demand on the Creditor's behalf.

Address

Tel. No. Ref No.

NOTES FOR CREDITOR

1. If the Creditor is entitled to the debt by way of assignment, details of the original Creditor and any intermediary assignees should be given in part B on page 3.
2. If the amount of debt includes interest not previously notified to the Company as included in its liability, details should be given, including the grounds upon which interest is charged. The amount of interest must be shown separately.
3. Any other charge accruing due from time to time may be claimed. The amount or rate of the charge must be identified and the grounds on which it is claimed must be stated.
4. In either case the amount claimed must be limited to that which has accrued due at the date of the demand.
5. If signatory of the demand is a solicitor or other agent of the Creditor, the name of his/her firm should be given.

N.B. The person making this Demand must complete the whole of this page, page 2 and parts A and B (as applicable) on page 3.

* Delete if signed by the Creditor himself.

1 (P.T.O

Form 11(a) continued

Particulars of Debt (These particulars must include **(a)** when the debt was incurred, **(b)** the consideration for the debt (or if there is no consideration the way in which it arose) and **(c)** the amount due as at the date of this demand).

NOTES FOR CREDITOR

1. If the Creditor is entitled to the debt by way of assignment, details of the original Creditor and any intermediary assignees should be given in part B on page 3.
2. If the amount of debt includes interest not previously notified to the Company as included in its liability, details should be given, including the grounds upon which interest is charged. The amount of interest must be shown separately.
3. Any other charge accruing due from time to time may be claimed. The amount or rate of the charge must be identified and the grounds on which it is claimed must be stated.
4. In either case the amount claimed must be limited to that which has accrued due at the date of the demand.
5. If signatory of the demand is a solicitor or other agent of the Creditor, the name of his/her firm should be given.

NOTE
If space is insufficient continue on reverse of page 3 and clearly indicate on this page that you are doing so.

2

Form 11(a) continued

Part A

The individual or individuals to whom any communication regarding this demand may be addressed is/are:

Name
(BLOCK LETTERS)

Address

Postcode

Telephone Number

Reference

Part B

For completion if the Creditor is entitled to the debt by way of assignment.

	Name	Date(s) of Assignment
Original Creditor		
Assignees		

How to comply with a Statutory Demand

If the Company wishes to avoid a winding-up Petition being presented it must pay the debt shown on page 1, particulars of which are set out on page 2 of this notice, within the period of **21 days** after its service upon the Company. Alternatively, the Company can attempt to come to a settlement with the Creditor. To do this the Company should:

- Inform the individual (or one of the individuals) named in Part A immediately that it is willing and able to offer security for the debt to the Creditor's satisfaction; *or*
- inform the individual (or one of the individuals) named in Part A immediately that it is willing and able to compound for the debt to the Creditor's satisfaction.

If the Company disputes the demand in whole or in part it should:

- contact the individual (or one of the individuals) named in Part A above immediately.

Remember! The Company has only 21 days after the date of service on it of this document before the Creditor may present a winding-up Petition.

3

Form 11(a) **continued**

Form 11(b) Statutory demand (individual)

Reproduced by kind permission of the Solicitor's Law Stationery Society

Form 6.1

Statutory Demand under section 268(1)(a) of the Insolvency Act 1986. Debt for Liquidated Sum Payable Immediately. (Rule 6.1)

WARNING

- This is an **important** document. You should refer to the notes entitled "How to comply with a Statutory Demand or have it set aside".
- If you wish to have this Demand set aside you must make application to do so **within 18 days** from its service on you.
- If you do not apply to set aside **within 18 days** or otherwise deal with this Demand as set out in the notes **within 21 days** after its service on you, you could be made bankrupt and your property and goods taken away from you.
- Please read the Demand and notes carefully. If you are in any doubt about your position you should seek advice **immediately** from a solicitor or your nearest Citizens Advice Bureau.

NOTES FOR CREDITOR

- If the Creditor is entitled to the debt by way of assignment, details of the original Creditor and any intermediary assignees should be given in part C on page 3.
- If the amount of debt includes interest not previously notified to the Debtor as included in the Debtor's liability, details should be given, including the grounds upon which interest is charged. The amount of interest must be shown separately.
- Any other charge accruing due from time to time may be claimed. The amount or rate of the charge must be identified and the grounds on which it is claimed must be stated.
- In either case the amount claimed must be limited to that which has accrued due at the date of the Demand.
- If the Creditor holds any security the amount of debt should be the sum the Creditor is prepared to regard as unsecured for the purposes of this Demand. Brief details of the total debt should be included and the nature of the security and the value put upon it by the Creditor, as at the date of the Demand, must be specified.
- If signatory of the Demand is a solicitor or other agent of the Creditor, the name of his/her firm should be given.

* Delete if signed by the Creditor himself.

DEMAND

To

Address

This Demand is served on you by the Creditor:

Name

Address

The Creditor claims that you owe the sum of £
full particulars of which are set out on page 2, and that it is payable immediately and, to the extent of the sum demanded, is unsecured.

The Creditor demands that you pay the above debt or secure or compound for it to the Creditor's satisfaction.

[The Creditor making this Demand is a Minister of the Crown or a Government Department, and it is intended to present a Bankruptcy Petition in the High Court in London.] [Delete if inappropriate].

Signature of individual

Name
(BLOCK LETTERS)

Date day of

*Position with or relationship to Creditor:
*I am authorised to make this Demand on the Creditor's behalf.

Address

Tel. No. Ref. No.

N.B. The person making this Demand must complete the whole of pages 1, 2 and parts A, B and C (as applicable) on page 3.

[P.T.O.

1

Form 11(b) continued

Particulars of Debt

(These particulars must include (a) when the debt was incurred (b) the consideration for the debt (or if there is no consideration the way in which it arose) and (c) the amount due as at the date of this demand).

NOTES FOR CREDITOR

- If the Creditor is entitled to the debt by way of assignment, details of the original Creditor and any intermediary assignees should be given in part C on page 3.
- If the amount of debt includes interest not previously notified to the Debtor as included in the Debtor's liability, details should be given, including the grounds upon which interest is charged. The amount of interest must be shown separately.
- Any other charge accruing due from time to time may be claimed. The amount or rate of the charge must be identified and the grounds on which it is claimed must be stated.
- In either case the amount claimed must be limited to that which has accrued due at the date of the Demand.
- If the Creditor holds any security the amount of debt should be the sum the Creditor is prepared to regard as unsecured for the purposes of this Demand. Brief details of the total debt should be included and the nature of the security and the value put upon it by the Creditor, as at the date of the Demand, must be specified.
- If signatory is a solicitor or other agent of the Creditor, the name of his/her firm should be given.

Note:
If space is insufficient continue on page 4 and clearly indicate on this page that you are doing so.

2

Form 11(b) continued

Part A
Appropriate Court for Setting Aside Demand

Rule 6.4(2) of the Insolvency Rules 1986 states that the appropriate Court is the Court to which you would have to present your own Bankruptcy Petition in accordance with Rule 6.40(1) and 6.40(2). In accordance with those rules on present information the appropriate Court is [the High Court of Justice] [County Court]
(address)

Any application by you to set aside this Demand should be made to that Court.

Part B
The individual or individuals to whom any communication regarding this Demand may be addressed is/are:

Name ....
(BLOCK LETTERS)

Address ....

....

....

Telephone Number ....

Reference ....

Part C
For completion if the Creditor is entitled to the debt by way of assignment.

	Name	Date(s) of Assignment
Original Creditor		
Assignees		

How to comply with a Statutory Demand or have it set aside (ACT WITHIN 18 DAYS)

If you wish to avoid a Bankruptcy Petition being presented against you, you must pay the debt shown on page 1, particulars of which are set out on page 2 of this notice, within the period of **21 days** after its service upon you. Alternatively, you can attempt to come to a settlement with the Creditor. To do this you should:

- inform the individual (or one of the individuals) named in Part B above immediately that you are willing and able to offer security for the debt to the Creditor's satisfaction; *or*
- inform the individual (or one of the individuals) named in Part B above immediately that you are willing and able to compound for the debt to the Creditor's satisfaction.

If you dispute the Demand in whole or in part you should:

- contact the individual (or one of the individuals) named in Part B immediately.

If you consider that you have grounds to have this Demand set aside or if you do not quickly receive a satisfactory written reply from the individual named in Part B whom you have contacted you should **apply within 18 days** from the date of service of this Demand on you to the appropriate Court shown in Part A above to have the Demand set aside.

Any application to set aside the Demand (Form 6.4 in Schedule 4 of the Insolvency Rules 1986) should be made within 18 days from the date of service upon you and be supported by an Affidavit (Form 6.5 in Schedule 4 to those Rules) stating the grounds on which the Demand should be set aside. The forms may be obtained from the appropriate Court when you attend to make the application.

> **Remember:** From the date of service on you of this document:
> (a) you have only **18 days** to apply to the Court to have the Demand set aside, and
> (b) you have only **21 days** before the Creditor may present a Bankruptcy Petition.

3

Form 11(b) **continued**

4

OYEZ The Solicitors' Law Stationery Society Ltd, Oyez House, 7 Spa Road, London SE16 3QQ

1996 Edition 8.98 T01356
5090337
* *

Insolvency-Bankruptcy 6.1

Alternative medicine

While the terms upon which a supplier agrees to grant credit generally remain the seller's decision alone (it is up to him or her whether to sell on those terms or not) a number of interrelated factors will determine how strongly the seller presses his or her case for early payment. These factors can be defined as follows:

1 The commercial edge which the supplier or the goods or services to be supplied have at any one time – that is to say, does demand exceed supply?
2 The value of the customer's business and the volume of sales which are likely.
3 The profitability of the sales envisaged when set against the cost of supplying the goods and services on credit terms.
4 The rate of turnover of the goods or services within the seller's market place, which in turn determines the capital requirements and the need for liquidity in the business.
5 The practices of the supplier's competition in the market.

In general terms the assumption raised in this book thus far has been that the buyer and seller are operating more or less on the basis of equality so that the normal UK terms which apply to the sale of goods, that is to say 30 days net, have been referred to.

On occasion, however, the seller may be in a stronger or weaker marketing position and may be able to insist upon more prompt terms of payment, or indeed may be forced to accept longer terms.

Letter 35 Letter requiring payment on order

Dear

Account No.
Balance Outstanding: £

Your account appears to have been persistently in arrears for a considerable period of time and the above balance has been overdue for [ ] weeks.

I regret to inform you that we will therefore be withdrawing your credit facilities for the time being and as a result must ask that any further orders placed with us are either:

1 Accompanied by payment in full in cash or by banker's draft.
2 Accompanied by payment by cheque to be cleared before delivery.
3 Despatched to you on a Cash on Delivery basis.

I do hope of course that this arrangement will only be temporary and that, following the payment of the above balance, we will be able to discuss a renewed credit facility soon.

Yours sincerely

Credit Manager

If the supplier is feeling particularly bullish he or she may insist on cash in advance, cash with order, cash before shipment or cash on delivery. **Letter 35** sets out an example of a letter where the supplier records the customer's persistent delay in payment and indicates that the supplier will be unable to provide further services or supplies unless payment in cash is made on order, or by cheque to be cleared before delivery or on a cash-on-delivery basis. This letter can be adapted to incorporate any of the terms mentioned above, provided of course that the supplier is in a strong enough position within his or her market to insist on those terms.

SMALL COMPANIES AND SERVICE COMPANIES

Small businesses have for many years suffered in the credit management stakes quite simply because the commercial leverage they are able to apply in obtaining prompt payment from their customers is substantially less than their larger competitors. In addition, because they are more likely to be newer businesses they are fighting to attain a market share and the price they have to pay is sometimes a degree of exploitation at the hands of their larger customers, who have the benefit of substantial purchasing power and are able to negotiate favourable terms with their suppliers.

As a result, some of the collection techniques advocated in this book may not be immediately appropriate for very small businesses who may have a small number of relatively high-value but low-risk customers. Such a company would be very reluctant indeed to stop the supply of its goods to a new but large customer who is promising further orders subject to satisfactory performance by the supplier. That reluctance would continue even if that customer were to prefer paying on 60-day terms rather than on 30-day terms previously agreed.

In those circumstances the small business clearly has to exercise a substantial degree of commercial judgment as to how far an important customer should be allowed to dictate terms. If he or she simply submits to all the demands the customer makes, then that customer's respect will quickly be lost and the supplier will be seen as the provider of an alternative means of finance for that customer's business.

On the other hand, having decided that the further orders on offer are worth a degree of flexibility in approach, there is no reason at all why the managers of the smaller business should not take a commercial decision which would allow their customer an extended period of credit, provided of course that the cost of that credit is built into their sales figures. At the very least that cost should be appreciated as an overhead of the business to be made up in some other way, perhaps by being built into the company's new pricing structure. In any event, having taken into account the commercial risks which are being accepted, and perhaps bearing in mind that such risks are part and parcel of getting a small business off the ground, the managers of that business must then ensure that they apply the guidelines which have been set out already in this book. Using the forms and letters which are provided they should, at the earliest possible opportunity, build for themselves a credit management system which is appropriate for their needs. In the meantime, there is no reason why they should not make their position perfectly clear to their customer, and an appropriate form of letter setting out the small company's position on receipt of an order from a large buyer is set out at **Letter 36**. By the gradual application of such a system and by ensuring that a continuing dialogue takes place between the smaller business and its larger customers, an element of mutual trust and respect can be established, so that eventually the larger company is persuaded to reduce its demands and to comply at least in part with the normal trading terms and collection procedures of its smaller colleague.

For different reasons, similar attitudes tend to prevail in the service industry where the suppliers, perhaps considering themselves to be involved in professional and therefore more personal relationships with their customers and

Letter 36 Letter from small company to major buyer

Dear

Many thanks for your order numbered [ ] dated [ ]. It is being dealt with now and the goods will be with you on the date requested.

The prices quoted to you are the keenest we can offer and so they have not been inflated with the cost of extended credit. To enable us to keep our charges low we would like to agree payment terms with you of 30 days from date of invoice.

Despite our terms and conditions which include interest surcharges on overdue accounts and the fact that the Late Payment of Commercial Debt (Interest) Act gives us the right to charge interest on overdue accounts, this is not something we want to do. We cannot see any value in 'fining' our own customers. We are a small company and cash flow is far more important to us than accumulating interest on our sales ledger. Prompt payment helps reduce charges and enables us to provide consistently good and uninterrupted service to our customers.

Will you please confirm that these payment terms are acceptable to you? I can then contact your bought ledger department to set up the account as we have agreed.

Thank you.

Yours sincerely

Director

clients, sometimes consider that the application of good credit management practices is to an extent 'ungentlemanly', 'pushy' or 'grasping', and as a result are unwilling either to impose payment terms and credit limits on their customers or to enforce those terms and limits when they are exceeded.

It is now apparent that the service industry sector of the UK economy has grown with remarkable rapidity over the past twenty years and now provides a major part of this country's GDP. Because the services provided are often not as tangible as goods delivered to an order, the client or customer can more easily query the value of the service and perhaps dispute the amounts he or she is being charged.

This is particularly true in the case of urgent services which are supplied without any opportunity for prior price quotation, credit checks or the agreement of specific terms for payment.

In such circumstances it is vital from the supplier's point of view that first the terms upon which the business is being done are emphasised at the earliest opportunity and second that he or she ensures that the customer appreciates the value of the service supplied and the degree of speed involved. This can only be done if a fee or rate of charge is agreed at the time the work is carried out or very shortly thereafter, and if an appropriate invoice is delivered quickly after the work has been completed. Clients of professional firms in particular have remarkably short memories when it comes to the amount of time and effort expended by their professional advisers on urgent matters, and if the billing of that work is left even for a month or two the client will often find great difficulty in remembering what the fuss was all about and why the fees claimed have become so apparently excessive.

Again, although particular circumstances may arise in which a service company may be prepared to take a degree of risk in providing services to a new or high-risk customer without full security for the fees to be charged, there is no real excuse for ignoring the basic principles of credit management which have been expounded in this book. Similarly, there is no reason at all why an appropriately flexible credit management system should not be created within such a business with terms for payment, conditions of sale and credit limits being agreed with regular customers and new clients alike in advance of the receipt of instructions. The various forms and letters set out in previous chapters, suitably adapted, are all perfectly usable by such companies and partnerships, but to cover requests for emergency services an additional letter as in **Letter 37** will undoubtedly be of assistance.

Letter 37

Letter from service company to client

Dear

Many thanks for appointing us to manage the [ ] project. Work will begin immediately and I will keep you informed at all stages of progress.

At our meeting this morning, because of the urgency of this matter, I forgot to discuss with you our terms of service. These are our fees and terms of payment. Other Terms of Business are shown overleaf.

Senior Managers	:	£ hourly
Junior Managers	:	£ hourly
Expenses and Outside Charges	:	These are defined in the Terms of Business overleaf and will be charged at cost

In this assignment it is likely that a Senior Manager will be involved for most of the time using the assistance of a Junior Manager when required.

Terms of payment are 30 days from the end of the month of invoice date. This applies for work completed in the period and interim invoices for work-in-progress. Will you please confirm these terms are acceptable to you.

Yours sincerely

Senior Manager

TIME FOR PAYMENT

Once the supplier has assessed the true cost of supplying credit to customers who seek it and has set that cost against the position of the business within his or her market place and the ability of these customers to obtain better credit facilities elsewhere, alternative forms of credit facilities may be agreed. These may be either weekly credit, which requires payment by a specified day in the following week, half-monthly or monthly credit, which requires payment in full of all supplies made in the relevant half-monthly or monthly period to be discharged by a specific date in the following month, or net seven prox, terms which, like monthly credit, requires payment by specific dates (say the 7th) of the following month.

The supplier and his or her customer may also agree on terms by which payment on an existing account can be discharged by instalments. **Letter 38** sets out the terms of a letter which can be used for this purpose (see also **Letter 23**). The letter confirms the balance currently due, the number of instalments to be agreed and the amount payable each month. It also reminds the customer that interest is due in accordance with the supplier's conditions of sale and sets out

Letter 38 Letter agreeing to payment of debt by instalments

Dear

Account No.
Balance Due: £

Following our recent discussions I am pleased to confirm that I am authorised to agree with you the payment of the above balance by [6] monthly instalments of £[ ] per month. Your payments will be made by postdated cheques and will include interest at the rate of [ ] per cent in accordance with the terms of our Conditions of Sale.

For the avoidance of doubt I confirm that the cheques will be dated and paid as follows:

Date	Principal sum	Interest	Total

I also confirm our agreement that in the event that any of these cheques are not promptly met by your bank on presentation then the whole amount remaining including interest up to that time will fall due without further demand and we reserve the right to issue court proceedings against you for the remaining balance as we see fit.

I am sure those steps will not be necessary, however, and I look forward to receiving your [6] cheques by [date]. Please confirm your agreement to these terms by signing the enclosed copy of this letter by way of acknowledgment and returning it to me with your cheques.

Yours sincerely

Credit Manager

I hereby acknowledge my company's indebtedness in the sum of £
and confirm the repayment of that sum under the terms set out above.

....

Director
For and on behalf of [ ] Limited

the full amount of the principal sum, plus interest, and total which remains. Then the customer is reminded that the agreement is granted as a concession and that in default of any one instalment being met the whole balance plus interest will immediately fall due.

Letter 39 can be used when an agreement is reached between the supplier and his or her customer that payment for a new order can also be made by instalments. In this example a percentage of the invoice value is required on order, on delivery, 30 days after delivery and 60 days after delivery, although of

Letter 39 Letter agreeing to payment for new order by instalments

Dear

Order No.
Total Value: £

I am pleased to be able to confirm that I have now obtained authority to accept your order on the basis [you have proposed] [we have discussed], namely that payment should be made by a series of instalments as follows:

On order:	25% of invoice value
On delivery:	25% of invoice value
30 days after delivery:	25% of invoice value
60 days after delivery:	25% of invoice value

The terms upon which I am authorised to accept the order are as follows:

1. In the event of any default in payment prior to delivery we reserve the right to cancel the order and to retain the amount then paid as a non-refundable deposit to compensate us for production and purchasing costs.
2. All instalments to be made post-delivery will be made without deduction or set-off in relation to any claim by you relating to the delivery, quality or condition of the goods.
3. In the event that any default is made in the payment of any instalment after delivery we reserve the right to claim the full contract price together with interest thereon under the terms of our Conditions of Sale and to take such steps as may be available to us to recover any balances due.
4. The terms of our Conditions of Sale (copy attached) will apply exclusively to this Order.

Please indicate your acceptance of these terms by signing the copy of this letter attached and returning it to me by [date].

Yours sincerely

I hereby confirm our order number [ ] subject to the conditions set out above.

Director
For and on behalf of [ ] Limited

course it is open to each supplier to insist upon the timing he or she requires. Again, it is firmly emphasised that in the event of any default in payment prior to delivery the supplier reserves the right to cancel and to retain the amount then paid as a non-refundable deposit. All instalments to be made after delivery should be made without deduction or set-off and in the event of any default at that time the supplier reserves the right to claim the full contract price, together with interest, under his or her conditions of sale.

The fact that the supplier's conditions of sale apply is repeated and the pur-

Letter 40 Letter agreeing to payment for part-delivery by instalments

Dear

Order No.
Total Value: £

I am pleased to confirm that following our recent discussions I have been able to obtain authority to accept your above order and, as requested, we are prepared to deliver by instalments and accept payment for each individual instalment on the following terms:

1 Notwithstanding our agreement to deliver by instalments and accept payment for each instalment as it is delivered, this order is to be treated as a single contract for all other purposes.
2 In the event of your default in payment for any instalment the full balance payable for the whole order will immediately fall due and we reserve all our rights in relation thereto.
3 The contract will in all other respects be governed exclusively by the attached terms of our Conditions of Sale.

Please confirm your receipt of and agreement to these terms by signing the copy of this letter attached and returning it to me by [date].

Yours sincerely

I acknowledge receipt of and accept the conditions attached to our order as set out above.

Director
For and on behalf of [ ] Limited

chaser is invited to confirm the order on those terms and to acknowledge the conditions being set. **Letter 40** provides a precedent by which the parties agree to arrange for deliveries under a single contract to be made by instalments and for payment under that contract to be made on a similar basis. The order number and the total value are confirmed and it is acknowledged that in spite of the fact that part-deliveries and part-payments are to be exchanged, the order is to be treated as a single contract for all other purposes. This affects the parties' rights to cancel the contract or to claim damages in the event of a default of a single instalment on delivery, and again it is emphasised that in the event of the buyer's default in payment of any instalment the full balance payable will fall due. In all other respects the supplier's conditions of sale will apply and again the purchaser is required to accept the conditions attached to the order by signing a copy of the letter and returning it to the supplier.

DISCOUNTS AND PENALTIES

Apart from demanding early cash payment or agreeing to payment by instalments, a supplier may decide to allow certain customers specific incentives to encourage early payment or alternatively extra charges may be imposed if payment is made after the time which is agreed. This 'carrot and stick' approach can be of assistance to your business provided that, in the event that discounts for early settlement are offered, an increase in turnover is anticipated and the costs of providing those discounts are calculated into your budgeted figures. Otherwise, every discount which is allowed will simply eat into your profit margins and may indeed outweigh the benefits you are obtaining in cash-flow terms. In addition, while you may deliberately wish such a discount to be seen as a positive benefit to your customer, you must not overlook the tendency for some to deduct the discount from their payments whether they have complied with the discount terms or not. This leaves you in a position where a small balance on each account remains due [say, 2.5 per cent] and a potential argument likely with an established customer. Alternatively a series of write-offs may be required for a number of small balances which consistently eat into your profit levels.

The use of the word 'penalty' should be avoided at all costs in your trading terms or in your correspondence with your customers. The reason for this is that a penalty, that is to say an unwarranted payment required without any reference to a genuine and reasonable pre-estimate of the loss anticipated by one party or another, is not enforceable under English law. What you do is to make a reasonable attempt to assess in advance the likely losses of one party or the other and to agree, for example in the event of the buyer's default, that he or she should pay to the seller a fixed liquidated sum which is expressed to provide that assessment and is acknowledged by both sides as being fair and reasonable.

Alternatively, the parties can agree either expressly in correspondence or by the adoption of the conditions of sale of one side or the other that a specific rate of interest is to apply from the date either when the invoice is delivered or the date upon which it becomes overdue. The starting point for the charging of interest is a matter of negotiation and agreement between the parties.

If you do decide to charge interest on overdue accounts, then you must again be careful to ensure that the level of interest to be charged is one which reflects your true intentions. It must not be so low as to encourage your customer to delay payment while accepting the charge for the facility on the basis that it is lower than the interest rate charged by the bank to his or her overdraft, but on the other hand it must not be so high as to be punitive and possibly unenforceable as a penalty as described above. The normal rates applied commercially during recent years have been 3 per cent or 4 per cent over the base rate of a particular clearing bank, or alternatively around 1.5 per cent per month.

Under the Late Payment of Commercial Debts (Interest) Act 1998, the statutory rate is currently 8 per cent above bank base rate. Accordingly, those sellers to whom the Act currently applies might choose to rely upon this statutory right to late payment interest or, alternatively, set a contractual rate for late payment interest up to the statutory rate without this provision being struck down as penal.

Letter 41 is a letter which can be used to confirm a rate of interest to be applied on new orders, thereby perhaps amending the conditions of sale under which the parties had previously traded. You should note that the seller again emphasises that his or her conditions of sale shall continue to apply in all other respects, but then goes on to put the amendments into effect in relation to all orders placed with the company from a specific date.

Letter 41 Letter confirming new rate of interest

Dear

Account No.

We have noticed during recent months that your account has fallen into arrears and that your payments for invoices have often been received some time after they have become overdue.

You will appreciate that such late payment results in interest and other costs being incurred by our company and, in an effort to defray those costs, we think it is reasonable that we should be entitled to charge interest on outstanding accounts from the date upon which they become overdue under our Conditions of Sale. You will recall from those conditions (copy attached) that our accounts are due for payment within 30 days and, to give you a reasonable amount of notice, we advise you that on all orders delivered by us after the first of next month it is our intention to charge interest on payments in respect of such orders as become overdue at the rate of 8% over the Base Lending Rate for the time being of [National Westminster] Bank Plc.

Clearly, we hope that by paying our invoices promptly in future such additional charges will not be necessary but, in any event, please acknowledge receipt of this letter by signing one copy and returning it to me.

Yours sincerely

Credit Manager

I hereby acknowledge receipt of the above letter and confirm our acceptance of its terms.

....

Director – for and on behalf of [ ] Limited

FACTORING AND INVOICE DISCOUNTING

These are methods by which a supplier of goods or services effectively sells his or her sales ledger from time to time to a third party for a price, that price being dependent upon the terms which are agreed between them. There are many different forms of factoring and each of the finance houses concerned which take on this style of corporate funding will have their own form of agreement setting out the terms which they prefer and the charges and methods of payment which they wish to apply.

The principles involved, however, are basically the same. The supplier remains responsible for delivery of the goods or services and the preparation and delivery of invoices. Copies of those invoices are usually sent to the factor who will maintain sales ledger records relating to those invoices. Having assessed the risk involved in the supplier's business, the factor will provide finance on the basis of all or part of the sales ledger which has been assigned, usually up to about 80 per cent of the value of indebtedness to the supplier which is shown by the face value of those invoices. While the agreed percentage is paid as soon as the invoices are assigned by the factor, the balance will only be paid or received by the supplier when the customer pays. This form of factoring may be disclosed to the supplier's customer or not depending on the supplier's preference. He or she may prefer, for example, that customers are not aware of the financial arrangements. The supplier may not like it to become general knowledge that he or she is raising working capital in this way and may therefore wish to retain responsibility for the collection of his or her own outstanding accounts.

On the other hand, some factors provide full credit management services including the maintenance of the sales ledger, collection of debts and protection against bad debts, of course for varying rates of charges. If the factor is to collect the debt, then it is important that the supplier informs his or her customers at the earliest opportunity of the new system which is being introduced and a letter as set out in **Letter 42** can be used for this purpose. This letter mentions that a credit review has taken place (which will probably have been inevitable if a decision to factor a company's debts has been taken) and notice is given as to the date upon which the factoring company will become responsible for the collection of outstanding accounts. The supplier specifies that from that date invoices delivered will be overprinted with the factor's name and address and reference number and requests that payments relating to those accounts should be delivered direct.

If the supplier is to retain control of the collection of his or her debts, the factor will inevitably set a series of rules and regulations with which the supplier must comply, dealing for example with the assessment of credit risks, the setting of credit limits, the application of terms of credit and the action to be taken on default. These disciplines can of course be extremely useful to the supplier to ensure that everything is in order and that the credit collection systems used are working effectively.

Letter 42 Letter advising of appointment of factoring agents

Dear

Your Account No.

I am pleased to advise you that following our recent Credit Review, we have decided that to enable us to improve our financial controls and the information we are able to provide to you, we have decided to engage the services of [ ] Factors Limited who will from [ ] be responsible for the collection of monies due from you on our invoices.

From that date our invoices will be delivered to you overprinted with a name, address and reference number at [ ] Factors Limited to whom full payment should be made. I should emphasise, however, that all other terms of our Conditions of Sale will continue to apply and any queries arising in relation to any of our invoices or our goods should continue to be addressed to me.

I do hope that you will be able to cooperate in the success of this new system and if there is any further information I can provide to you in connection with it please do not hesitate to let me know.

Yours sincerely

Credit Manager

Invoice discounting is in fact a type of undisclosed factoring where the supplier remains responsible for the collection of all his or her own invoices but upon the assignment of the business sales ledger receives a percentage of its value. The credit management services involved in this system tend to be fewer, but the discounting agency will undoubtedly wish to satisfy itself that the supplier's credit procedures are sound before agreeing to enter into such an arrangement. In any event, under the terms of an invoice discounting agreement the supplier will usually be obliged to undertake to the factor that in the event that his or her customers do not pay, the supplier will refund the amounts advanced with interest. Where the supplier remains liable to refund the amounts advanced, the arrangement is known as 'recourse' factoring or invoice discounting. It is of course possible to negotiate with a factoring company a 'non-recourse' factoring or invoicing discounting arrangement, but the cost of these is likely to be higher, in line with the additional risk to the factoring company.

The ultimate objective of these systems of course is to improve the supplier's cash flow by enabling him or her to recover at least a proportion of the money due very quickly, passing over to the factor payments relating to the factored invoices as they come in while being charged interest on accounts remaining overdue beyond an agreed period. Depending upon the terms of the agreement reached, the supplier may remain responsible for any very late payments, bad debts or write-offs which may be required.

The effect of such a system is not as may be suspected, namely to confuse the process of cash collection and provide another perhaps undesirable tier of credit management. The existence of a third party between the supplier and his or her customer can often impose a useful discipline on the supplier which can be provided by the factor's objective approach and his or her experience in credit management generally. By imposing the rules and restrictions mentioned above, factoring can in fact instill many of the good habits advocated in this book and many of the systems and controls which all businesses require in order to ensure a proper inflow of cash into their organisation.

USING COLLECTION AGENCIES

In the past, some debt collection agencies had a rather poor image which was brought about by a minority who adopted mildly threatening door-to-door techniques in the collection of mainly consumer or small business debts. During recent years, however, agencies have become significantly more professional and sophisticated in dealing with larger-scale collection, either supplementing the services of their clients' own credit management teams or taking over the functions of such departments altogether.

The advantage in employing the services of such agencies is that a variety of services can be provided to meet the needs of the supplier. The suppliers can either pass individual claims to the agents for collection or pass debts which have been outstanding for a specific time (say 60 days). Alternatively they can instruct the agent to deal with the whole of the sales ledger from the date of delivery of the invoices, or to recover payment on invoices over a specific amount, without feeling any loss of control. The decision to instruct an agency will depend, however, on whether you consider that they can provide an additional service and benefit which your credit team and your solicitors cannot.

Since many agencies accept instructions on a full contingency basis, that is to say no collection – no fee, and charge a fee which is based on a percentage of the debt recovered, the supplier is then faced with the encouraging prospect of incurring fees only against cash actually received. Once the supplier has been able to assess his or her company's own collection performance and compare it with the performance of his or her agents, the reasonableness of the charges being applied can be calculated, as can the extent to which those charges are eating into the supplier's profit margins and thereby requiring adjustment to his or her sales figures. Collection agency staff are trained and experienced in the specific skills required to negotiate payment of overdues both by telephone and by letter. The use of these skills – if you do not have them 'in house' – gives your company the opportunity to increase profitability.

Collection agencies can also act as a useful method of monitoring and reporting back on cases when court proceedings have become necessary. They may undertake collection by telephone up to a certain point in time and they can provide a first and alternative step for the supplier's credit management team before costly and time consuming litigation is begun. An approach by a third party to your late paying customers will put additional pressure on them to settle outstanding accounts.

When deciding to instruct a debt collection agency it is important to set out clearly the authority which your agent has and the steps which you require him or her to take on your behalf.

Letter 43 sets out the terms which you may wish to use as a checklist in relation to the provision of services to be agreed. You will see that in this case the supplier has given:

1 a clear indication as to the age of the debts to be passed for collection;
2 the methods (a first letter followed by telephone calls) by which collection attempts are to be made;
3 the fact that all contact with customers should be conducted in the most courteous terms possible;
4 the rate of the agent's success fee;
5 the method by which payments received are to be transmitted to the suppliers.

Letter 43 Letter to collection agency confirming terms and authority

Dear

I am writing following our recent discussions to confirm the terms upon which my company wishes to instruct your agency in relation to the collection of unpaid invoices as follows:

1 We will instruct you by delivering copies of our invoices when they become [10] days overdue under the terms of our Conditions of Sale, that is 40 days after invoice date.
2 You will endeavour to collect the amounts due by a first letter requiring payment within seven days, to be followed in the event of non-payment by such telephone calls and follow-up letters as you see fit.
3 All correspondence and discussions with our customers must be conducted in the most courteous terms possible and any queries in relation to our accounts or complaints relating to delivery or the quality of our goods must be reported to us at once.
4 In the event that you are successful in collecting any unpaid invoice you will be entitled to a fee amounting to [ ]% of the gross value of that invoice, such fee to be deducted from the value of that invoice when paid.
5 Payments to us in respect of monies received by you shall be made immediately upon successful clearance through your bank and shall be accompanied by a full report setting out the name of our customer, the invoice numbers in respect of which payments have been received, the amount of your commission and the net amount paid to us.

Letter 43 continued

6* In the event that you are unsuccessful in recovering the balances payable in respect of our invoices within [60] days from the date when any such invoice fell due you shall apply to us, on a form to be agreed, for authority to instruct solicitors to write a seven-day letter before action to the relevant debtor.

7* In the event that such letter before action receives no response you shall apply to us for authority to issue proceedings accordingly.

8* For the sake of clarity we should confirm that upon the instruction of solicitors to issue a letter before action your fee, in the event of recovery, shall be reduced to [ ]% of the total invoice price.

9* We reserve the right to be consulted in connection with any instructions given to solicitors in relation to these matters and to require them to report to us direct in relation to any defence or counterclaim which may be raised in relation to our invoices.

Please indicate your acceptance of these terms by signing the copy letter attached and returning it to me within seven days.

Yours sincerely

Credit Manager

We hereby accept your instructions in connection with the recovery of unpaid invoices in accordance with the terms set out above.

Director

**NB: Clauses 6–9 apply only where a company will use the collection agency's solicitors. If not, then after the [60] day period, the account should be passed back to the company.*

The timescale within which unpaid invoices are to be passed for legal action is set out and the supplier reserves the right to be consulted in relation to any instructions given to solicitors or in relation to any other point arising in the conduct of the proceedings.

Letter 44 advises your customers that a collection agency has been appointed to deal with overdue invoices. Your ultimate objective is to maintain your margins of profitability by keeping down to a minimum the cost to your company of extended periods of credit or the cost of repeated bad debts, and you are in effect using your collection agency as a cost-effective tool for that purpose. The end result to your customers if your tactics are successful is to keep down your

Letter 44

Letter to customer advising appointment of collection agency

Dear

Your Account No:

I am writing to advise you that following our recent Credit Control Review, in order to improve our services to you and to improve our response rate in relation to any queries that may arise on our invoices, we have decided to instruct [ ] Collectors Limited to deal with all of our invoices which become overdue under the terms of our Conditions of Sale.

This means that in relation to any of our invoices which have not been paid by you or have not been the subject of a legitimate query in relation to our accounts or a justifiable complaint in connection with delivery or the quality of our goods under the terms of those Conditions, [ ] Collectors Limited will become responsible for the recovery of overdue accounts up to and including the issue of court proceedings.

I am sure that such steps will not be necessary in the case of your account and of course if you have any particular query to raise on our invoices then I would still invite you to contact me direct before they become overdue.

Yours sincerely

Credit Manager

overheads and as a result to reduce the cost to your customers of your products and services. This may be something that you wish to emphasise in this particular letter.

FOREIGN CLAIMS

If you are involved from time to time in exporting goods abroad then clearly you will find it to your advantage to seek some form of secure payment from your customer. Your objective will be to avoid the inconveniences and delays which can arise as a result of the distances involved, language problems and the complexities of exchange controls and varying currency rates. During recent years, however, many foreign importers have become more reluctant to provide the traditional forms of security which have tended to become more expensive and thus eat into the importers' profit margins. Irrevocable and confirmed letters of credit, clean bills of exchange drawn on a buyer, the use of export credit insurance and finance arrangements involving any of these schemes, while providing the security sought, can, on occasion, give rise to additional administrative expense and cause delay in concluding an agreement, which in times of tight trading conditions both the exporter and his or her importer may wish to avoid.

Quite often the only way of reaching an agreement on the supply of goods or services is to trade on normal UK terms, thus providing the customer with a period of credit without security for payment at all. In those circumstances delinquent accounts are bound to arise and the time may come when the efforts of your credit management team and possibly their agents in the relevant country will prove fruitless. You may then have to consider whether to begin court proceedings abroad to recover the amounts due.

When you make the decision to sue, there are usually two courses open to you, subject to any express exclusive jurisdiction clause contained in the sale contract. You can either issue your claim in the jurisdiction of the courts of England and Wales, and provided there are reciprocal arrangements for the enforcement of any judgment obtained as a result in the jurisdiction where your debtor's assets are located, then the entry of a judgment there and the enforcement of that judgment may proceed fairly promptly.

The alternative is to begin your proceedings abroad, choosing as mentioned the country in which the debtor has his or her assets, in the hope that by prompt action on the part of your lawyers in that jurisdiction the full amount of your claims can be recovered. Before deciding to take any legal action in a foreign jurisdiction, however, you should be aware of a number of factors as follows:

1 the varying degrees of efficiency (and the lack of it!) of the legal systems in different countries in different parts of the world;
2 the varying timescales involved in such proceedings from the date of issue, and the promptness with which the steps in an action can be dealt with;
3 the varying degrees of quality between legal practices and indeed individual lawyers in various countries and the degree of urgency which is placed by the legal profession in some countries on the affairs of their clients;
4 to some extent the attitude of the courts in certain jurisdictions to claims by foreigners against nationals of their own country, and in addition the adverse view taken occasionally in relation to the enforcement of judgments entered abroad;
5 the wide variation in costs and charging rates involved in taking proceedings in various countries, particularly in Europe and the United States, and the basis on which these charges are made (for example, contingency, percentage or fixed fee).

For all these reasons it is important that sufficient research is carried out before formally instructing a lawyer abroad to take proceedings on your behalf. You may wish to write in the manner set out in **Letter 45** which again is a checklist of the areas you would wish to cover in an initial enquiry about the judicial system of the relevant country, in so far as it relates to the recovery of debts, charges likely

Letter 45 Letter to foreign lawyer

Dear Sir or Madam

Debtor Company:
Amount Outstanding: £

We wish to recover the sum of £[ ] from the above company whose principal place of business is within the jurisdiction of your courts. We are concerned to ensure that the recovery of the sum due to us is effected as quickly and as economically as possible and we would therefore be grateful if you could let us have your replies to the following queries:

1 Do you have a standard or a scale fee in relation to debt recovery work? If so please let us have particulars.
2 If you do not operate a scale system could you please let us know your hourly rates for such work and an estimate of the cost of recovery on the basis that no defence is lodged to our claim.
3 Please let us know the timescales involved in relation to the recovery of such an amount, again on the basis that no defence is raised by the above company. Do your courts have a system for application for summary judgment even if some form of defence or complaint is indicated?
4 Please let us have a note of the court fees payable on the issue of proceedings together with the various steps involved in a court action, and let us have a note of the recoverable costs which may be awarded against a debtor in the event that your proceedings are successful.
5 Do your courts recognise and enforce judgments properly obtained in the English courts?
6 If they do, please let us have an estimate of the costs you would be likely to incur in taking such enforcement proceedings.
7 Please let us know how long each of the following actions is likely to take:
   (a) issuing proceedings, entering default judgment, enforcement of judgment;
   (b) issuing proceedings, defence of action, judgment at trial;
   (c) registration of English judgment, enforcement of that judgment.

Your prompt response would be appreciated.

Yours faithfully

Credit Manager

to be applied and the timescales involved. You would wish to find out if any short cuts can be taken (for example, an application for summary judgment) and whether it would be quicker for you to obtain your judgment in the United Kingdom before enforcing it in the foreign jurisdiction, or whether the commencement of proceedings in that jurisdiction is likely to be more worthwhile.

Once you have obtained further detailed answers to the questions you have raised, and have been given some idea, perhaps by the timing of the response you have received from the foreign lawyer of your choice, as to the degree of urgency with which he or she is going to pursue the claim on your behalf, you may then wish formally to instruct that lawyer to begin action to recover the debt which is due to you. The question of 'which lawyer' will inevitably arise and to find a suitable practitioner who deals with such collection work you may wish to consult your own lawyer in the United Kingdom, the British Chamber of Commerce or the consulate in the country concerned.

Again, it may be wise for you to set out in detail the exact steps that you wish to be taken and the basis upon which your instructions are being given. **Letter 46** can be used as a precedent for a letter giving those instructions, acknowledging the rates of charge and timescales to be applied and enclosing the relevant order forms, conditions of sale, invoices and correspondence with your debtor company. You should also set out exactly the issues between you so that your advisers are able to inform you from the outset as to any particular problems that are likely to arise.

Letter 46 Letter to foreign lawyer confirming instructions

Dear

Many thanks for your letter of [ ]. I am grateful to you for the information you have provided in relation to your court system, details regarding your rates of charge, and the timescales involved in the court procedures in your country.

I would be grateful if you could take immediate steps to recover the balances due to us in this matter as follows:

1 Please issue a seven-day letter before action requiring immediate payment to you of the full balance outstanding.
2 If you receive no response please take immediate proceedings in your courts to obtain judgment and to enforce that judgment against the debtor.
3 In the event that any query is raised on our account or indication of a defence or counterclaim is raised by the defendant company, please let us have full particulars at once.
4 Please keep us informed as to all fees and disbursements involved in the action as they are incurred.

To enable you to proceed I enclose the following documents:

1 copy order and acknowledgement setting out our Conditions of Sale;
2 copy invoice and statements showing the full amounts due;
3 copy correspondence with the debtor company showing its acknowledgement of that indebtedness and indicating that no queries have arisen in relation to the account or the goods delivered.

I look forward to hearing from you in confirmation as soon as your action has begun.

Yours sincerely

Credit Manager

Conclusion

Having looked at the various methods that may be open to you by which an efficient credit management and cash collection system can be devised and having considered which suits the particular needs of your business, what are the main lessons to be learned to ensure that the efficiency of that system and its contribution to the profitability to your business are to be sustained?

The most important element is the recognition by the leaders of any commercial organisation that the control of credit and collection of cash is vital to its future prosperity. This must be backed up by a commitment to support the credit management team in their duties. While that commitment must be balanced against the resources required by the organisation's production, marketing and sales staff, on no account should the efforts of your credit managers be overridden by a drive for orders, turnover and paper profits – unless of course the true costs and implications of such a policy are entirely taken into account.

The acceptance of a credit management philosophy will involve the provision of the resources necessary to carry out the credit control function. The level of resources will depend upon the size and nature of the organisation involved but the bare minimum requirement should be the recognition of the credit manager's true role and authority within the business and the provision of the basic tools required to enable him or her to do the job.

These will include the opportunity to communicate authoritatively with his or her peers in other divisions of the business and to have a major say in all management decisions which affect his or her particular domain. The credit manager must also be given a free hand to set up a credit control policy and system which will, of necessity, impinge upon those other divisions to some degree. For example, if the credit manager's query/complaint procedures require prompt replies from the design or production teams, then the leaders of those teams must back those requirements and ensure that staff comply. If the system requires all sales documentation from quotation to invoice to carry copies of the business's Conditions of Sale and to exclude all other terms of business, then the sales director should support and enforce that requirement. If the credit manager insists upon regular statements of account being sent out to customers confirming balances currently due or imminently to become due, then the accounts team should provide their support in that task.

In other words, every effort should be made to ensure that the credit management and cash collection philosophy is engendered from the top of each organisation down the line-management structure and into the basic thinking of each division or department which has anything at all to do with the financial operation of the business.

Once such policies are accepted and put into place, there should be little difficulty in ensuring that the credit management team obtain the resources they require to carry out their job efficiently. Part of that requirement will of course involve initial and continued training of the credit management staff to enable them to use properly the tools and resources with which they have been provided. That training will involve assessing the terms upon which business is done, learning how to identify problems within a customer's own business, examining methods by which personal relationships between the credit management team and their customers can be enhanced, and learning techniques to ensure that, at every opportunity, the claims and demands of your business are satisfied at the earliest opportunity and, if possible, ahead of your own competitors and other claimants.

This book should help those involved at every level of commercial life to recognise their role in the credit function of their business. By accepting the importance of cash collection and repeating that message as often as required, and by emphasising the cost to the business of delayed payments and bad debts, you will find that very quickly the whole culture of your business can change from being one in which its general practices are lax and open to exploitation, to one which is geared towards efficiency at all levels and the promotion of quality services and products at every opportunity.

Only by the continued support for that philosophy, however, by the regular provision of the required resources and by the repetition of the organisation's clarion call that cash is its life's blood will sustained success be achieved.

Glossary

Administrative receiver: appointed by a creditor under a specific power arising under the terms of a fixed or floating charge. The receiver's duty is to realise the value of the asset charged for the benefit of his creditor/client. A company can continue to trade while in receivership but it cannot prevent a petition for its winding-up being presented to the court.

Agent: a person authorised expressly or by implication to act for another, called the principal, who is, as a result of the authority delegated by him, bound by the acts of the agent.

Bankruptcy: an individual debtor by reason of some act or circumstance indicating a failure or inability to meet his or her liabilities may be adjudged 'bankrupt' by the High Court or by a County Court. The bankrupt's property vests in his or her trustee in bankruptcy upon the making of an order and severe restrictions are placed upon his or her commercial activities.

Bill of exchange: defined by Bills of Exchange Act 1882, s. 1 as an unconditional order in writing, addressed by one person (the drawer) to another (the drawee and afterwards acceptor), signed by the person giving it, requiring the person to whom it is addressed to pay on demand, or at a fixed or determinable future time, a sum certain in money to, or to the order of, a specified person or to bearer (the payee).

Bill of lading: a receipt from a carrier given to a shipper or consignor, undertaking to deliver the goods upon payment of the freight, to the person described in the bill. The delivery of this document to the consignee is sufficient to transfer property in the goods. It is a document of title and a document of carriage.

Charging order: a form of proceedings to enforce a judgment (*q.v.*) which attaches to property, normally land or shares, owned by the debtor. The charging order operates like a mortgage in that it is usually used to secure payment by instalments. Upon default an order for sale may be made.

Conditions of sale: the contractual terms, usually in writing, upon which goods are sold and services supplied.

County Court: the County Courts since June 1991 have jurisdiction to hear all claims valued up to £50,000. From 26 April 1999, under the new Civil Procedure Rules, there are different procedures applicable to claims, depending on their value, as follows:

1 small claims track: covering all claims up to £5,000;
2 fast track: covering all claims between £5,000 and £15,000;
3 multi-track: covering all claims above £15,000.

Claims of £15,000 and above may be brought in the High Court but if the claim is contested and is for less than £50,000 it will be transferred down to the County Court.

Debenture: a document recording the indebtedness of one party to the other, containing a promise to repay and by way of security for that promise a floating charge over a company's assets.

Discounts:
either: (1) an allowance made to bankers or others for advancing money on bills of exchange before they become due

or (2) an allowance frequently made at the settlement of accounts, by way of deduction from the amount payable.

Document of title: a document enabling the person in possession of it to deal with the property described in it in any way as if they were the owner.

Enforcement: once a debt has been sued for successfully and judgment (*q.v.*) entered against the debtor there are various methods of physically recovering the money and those are enforcement methods. Examples are instructing bailiffs to distrain, charging orders, attachment of earnings, garnishee proceedings.

Fixed charge: a charge over a specific asset or type of asset, e.g. machinery, property, book debts, etc.

Floating charge: a charge created by a company over all company assets for the time being. The creditor has no immediate right over the assets but upon crystallisation of the charge he or she can enforce against any or all of the assets covered by the charge.

Garnishee proceedings: a form of proceedings to enforce a judgment upon money owed to or goods of a debtor held by a third party, e.g. money held in a bank account.

Gearing: accounting ratio of money borrowed compared with unencumbered capital. A company is said to be highly geared if a high proportion of their working capital is borrowed rather than invested.

Guarantee: a promise by one person to carry out the contractual commitments of another in the event of default. Must be in writing.

High Court: this court has jurisdiction to hear all claims without limitation. There are several district registries of the High Court throughout the country with the Central Office being at the Royal Courts of Justice in the Strand, London.

Indemnity: a promise to compensate another for a wrong-doing, expense or loss incurred. To be distinguished from a guarantee (*q.v.*) which relates to the obligations of another and may not be a primary obligation.

Insolvency: an inability to pay debts as they fall due, or where a debtor's total assets are exceeded by his or her liabilities. The law in this area is regulated by the Insolvency Act 1986.

Joint and several: when two or more persons declare themselves jointly and severally bound they make themselves liable to a separate and individual action as well as joint action in the event of default. If one person is pursued for the whole debt he can claim a contribution from the others.

Judgment: an order of the court in civil cases and in particular the award sought by the parties at the end of an action.

Liquidation: the term used to describe the winding up of a company usually by reason of an inability to pay its debts, regulated by the Insolvency Act 1986. It involves the realisation of the company's assets and the distribution of the proceeds to its creditors.

Registered office: the address of a company at which all documents must be served, in order for service to be effective. It is recorded at Companies House and can be found by referring to company headed paper or carrying out a company search.

Retention of title clause: also known as a 'Romalpa clause' it is a clause reserving the seller's title to the goods until those goods are fully paid for. It imposes a duty of care in respect of the goods on the buyer and purports to entitle the seller to recover the goods or trace the proceeds of sale.

Security: collateral provided by a debtor to support his or her promise to pay. A creditor may require some rights over valuable property in order to lend or supply, e.g. a charge over land. The security will be used to satisfy that creditor in the event of default.

Set-off: a form of defence whereby a debtor may acknowledge the claimant's demand but pleads his own claim in order to extinguish the claimant's demands either in full or in part.

Trading address: the address of the company where business is carried on if different from the registered office and where the company's assets are likely to be found.

Unsecured creditor: a creditor who has no security for his debt and will therefore rank with other unsecured creditors on an equal basis with no preference in the event of a liquidation or bankruptcy.

Waiver: the abandonment of a right by one party so that afterwards he or she is prevented from claiming it. It is possible to waive rights by conduct or by express agreement.

Warranties: promises or covenants offered usually by a seller to a buyer to describe the goods or services offered and the remedies available to the buyer in the event of default.

Useful contact addresses and telephone numbers

Bankruptcy Association of GB
4 Johnson Close
Abraham Heights
Lancaster LA1 5EU
Tel: 01524 64305

British Bankers Association
10 Lombard Street
London EC3V 9EL
Tel: 0207 623 4001

Civil Court Users Association
Orchard Court
Wellesbourne
Warwickshire
CV35 9JB
Tel: 01789 472195

Companies House
Crown Way
Maindy
Cardiff CF4 3UZ
Tel: 01222 383588

Consumer Credit Trade Association
159–163 Great Portland Street
London W1N 5FD
Tel: 0207 636 7564
Fax: 0207 323 0096

Council of Mortgage Lenders
3 Savile Row
London W1X 1AF

Credit Card Research Group
2 Ridgmount Street
London WC1E 7AA
Tel: 0207 436 9937

Credit Industry Fraud Avoidance Scheme
173–175 Cleveland Street
London W1P 5PE
Tel: 0207 383 0210

Credit AON
13 Grosvenor House
London SW1X 7HH
Tel: 0207 235 3550

Credit Services Association
Ensign House
56 Thorpe Road
Norwich
Norfolk NR1 1RY
Tel: 01603 629105

Department of Trade and Industry
1 Victoria Street
London SW1H 0ET
Tel: 0207 215 5000
e-mail:
dti.enquiries@imsv.dti.gov.uk
www.dti.gov.uk

EULER Trade Indemnity plc
1 Canada Square
London E14 5DX
Tel: 0207 512 9333
Fax: 0207 512 9186
www.tradeindemnity.com

Factors and Discounters Association
c/o Boston House
The Little Green
Richmond
Surrey TW9 1QE
Tel: 0208 332 9955

Finance & Leasing Association
15–19 Imperial House
Kingsway
London WC2B 6UN
Tel: 0207 836 6511

The Insolvency Service
PO Box 203
21 Bloomsbury Street
London WC1B 3QW
Tel: 0207 637 1110

Institute of Credit Management
The Water Mill
Station Road
South Luffenham, Oakham
Leics 8NB
Tel: 01780 722900
Fax: 01780 721333

Monopolies and Mergers Commission (MMC)
New Court
48 Carey Street
London WC2A 2JT
Tel: 0207 324 1467
e-mail: mmc@gtnet.gov.uk
www.mmc.gov.uk

National Consumer Credit Federation
98–100 Holme Lane
Sheffield
S/Yorks S6 4JW
Tel: 0114 234 8101

Office of the Data Protection Registrar
Wycliffe House
Water Lane
Wilmslow
Cheshire SK9 5AF
Tel: 01625 545700
e-mail:
data@wycliffe.demon.co.uk
www.open.gov.uk/dpr/dprhome.
htm

Office of Fair Trading
Field House
Breams Buildings
London EC4A 1PR
Tel: 0207 211 8000
www.oft.gov.uk

Scottish Consumer Credit Association
Delta Vouchers Ltd
105 North High Street
East Lothian
EH21 6JE
Tel: 0131 665 2261

Society of Practitioners of Insolvency
Halton House
20–23 Holborn
London EC2N 2JE
Tel: 0207 831 6563

Index

Index entries are to page numbers, those in italic referring to Letters, Forms and Documents.

Lightning Source UK Ltd.
Milton Keynes UK
UKOW06f1140121113

220882UK00011B/773/P

9 780273 644729